Praise for *Kingdom Citizen*

As Christians, sometimes our citizenship brings tough decisions our way: we don't want to let an election, policy decision, or court ruling steal our joy in Christ, but then we don't want to check out of the process either because we're called to be salt and light. In this book, Dr. Evans provides a well-reasoned, Bible-based picture of what our citizenship should look like from a kingdom perspective. In this culture that is often confused, Tony's message will challenge you to live more radically for God and His kingdom, and truly make a difference in your community.

—CAREY CASEY
National Center for Fathering

We must be completely dependent upon the Lord to strengthen our obedience to His Word and live it out before unbelievers that are watching the nations implode. Tony Evans has struck a chord in his timely book *Kingdom Citizen* as he speaks to the heart of the church in America. You will be challenged and convicted as you consider the Bible's charge for Christians to live as citizens of Heaven while on our journey through a strange and alien land.

—REV. FRANKLIN GRAHAM
President/CEO, Billy Graham Evangelistic
Association and Samaritan's Purse

At a time when so many Christians are feeling dismayed about our nation's moral and spiritual condition, Tony Evans turns our attention to where it belongs: on our sovereign and merciful God who calls us to be faithful ambassadors of truth in every realm, including the public square. This book is a must-read for every believer longing to know what biblical citizenship looks like.

—JIM DALY
President and CEO, Focus on the Family

KINGDOM CITIZEN

TONY EVANS

KINGDOM CITIZEN

YOUR ROLE IN REBUILDING
A BROKEN NATION

Focus on the Family and the accompanying logo and design are federally registered trademarks of Focus on the Family, 8605 Explorer Drive, Colorado Springs, CO 80920.

All Scripture quotations have been taken from the *New American Standard Bible*®. Copyright © 1960, 1962, 1963, 1968, 1971, 1972, 1973, 1975, 1977, 1995 by The Lockman Foundation. Used by permission. (www.Lockman.org).

The use of material from or references to various websites does not imply endorsement of those sites in their entirety. Availability of websites and pages is subject to change without notice.

Cover design and cover photo by Michael Harrigan

Library of Congress Cataloging-in-Publication Data for this title can be found at www.loc.gov.

ISBN 978-1-58997-893-5

Printed in the United States of America
22   21   20   19   18   17   16
7   6   5   4   3   2   1

CONTENTS

INTRODUCTION

In recent years, American politics have become more polarized than ever before. Political parties are divided, families are split, friendships are endangered, races are in conflict, and Christians like you are caught in the middle of heated discussions and disagreements.

Some believers are strongly determined about their choices, while others are confused and overwhelmed. Many fear for the future of our country, communities, and families. Most are seeking guidance based on God's Word and His promises for us. That's how this book came to be.

I want to help you answer God's call for you as a kingdom citizen—an individual and a member of the body of Christ. God's Word offers a broad vision, enabling you to fill this role even in a secular society. By understanding eternal principles, you will be equipped to move through contentious political seasons and learn to make biblical decisions that direct your choices and actions well into the future.

Unfortunately, far too many Christians operate as one of two extremes. They are either so heavenly minded that they are no earthly good or so earthly minded that they are no heavenly good. Kingdom citizens understand their role is to be heavenly minded so that they do good on earth. Kingdom citizens engage the world from a distinctly biblio-centric worldview without becoming worldly. They operate in the world without allowing themselves to be contaminated by the world. Kingdom citizens enter this world like scuba divers enter the ocean—with a tank on their backs. They take with them the life-giving presence and power of God's Word and Spirit in order to effectively function in an environment that is not their real home. Kingdom citizens recognize that personal conversion should also affect culture since Christ claims authority over heaven and earth and His followers are to disciple the nations (Matthew 28:19-20).

A kingdom citizen consistently models the Micah mandate which says, "He has told you, O man, what is good; And what does the Lord require of you but to do justice, to love kindness, And to walk humbly with your God?" (Micah 6:8)

You can further apply *Kingdom Citizen* concepts in your own life by working through the questions in the back of the book. You might also use them with friends and family members as discussion-starters for thought-provoking conversations.

Kingdom Citizen includes prayers from Christian leaders who share hope for healing a broken nation, trusting God for His power and grace in each of our lives. I am thankful for their voices and their faith in these times of challenge and change.

1

SEE THAT MESS?
BLAME ME

As we examine what is happening in our culture and country today, we see the continuous demise of our quality of life in virtually every area. Whether it's morality, crime, family, race relations, or education, every area of life has been marked by decline. The cultural colds of the 1980s turned into the pneumonia of the 1990s, which led to a cardiac arrest in the 2000s and beyond. The reason—as we will discover throughout our time together in these pages—is that there can be no social revitalization without appropriate theological application.

We cannot fix our communities, neighborhoods, families, crime, injustice, entertainment, or even our nation anthropologically unless there is first the proper theological understanding of the relationship of God to culture. And, more importantly, we must understand the relationship of God to His own people within that culture as His kingdom representatives—His kingdom citizens. A kingdom citizen is *a visible, verbal follower of Jesus Christ who consistently applies the principles of heaven to the concerns of the culture.*

Now if you don't believe me, ask the leaders of the former Soviet Union who spent seventy years telling us God does not exist. They established an atheistic system that left God out, only to discover years later that they had created a bankrupt republic. When a culture departs from God, its sociology must, by necessity, deteriorate.

The deterioration we are facing in our nation today is primarily related to the absence of God and the resultant absence of a thoroughly biblical worldview. We do not have a kingdom-minded foundation.

The Cracks Are Not the Problem

My wife, Lois, and I live in the same house we have lived in for more than thirty-five years. It is a modest home in an older neighborhood. We like it; it is comfortable. It's home. But if you know anything about Texas at all, you know that due to the extreme heat and often-relentless bursts of rain, the ground can shift. This is never good for a house. Our problems started early on.

A good while back, I noticed some fissures had appeared on one of the inside walls of our home. It wasn't long before I called in a painter to patch them up with plaster and repaint the wall. After he had finished, everything looked as good as new.

Unfortunately, though, about a month later the same cracks began to reappear. Except this time, they came back with a vengeance, bringing along smaller, spider-web cracks surrounding the originals. Assuming the last painter had done a poor job, I called another one who could really fix it this time. After the new painter arrived and looked at the cracks on my wall, he turned to me and said, "I can't help you."

"Why can't you help me?" I replied, confused.

"Because you don't have a problem with cracks on your wall."

I looked at the cracks on my wall then turned to the painter again—yes, the same painter who was telling me I didn't have a problem with cracks on my wall. Then I turned back to the cracks on my wall.

Your problem is that you have a shifting foundation.

He could see the frustration on my face, so he continued, "Tony, those are cracks on your wall. I'm not denying it. But the cracks are not your problem. Your problem is that you have a shifting foundation. Your foundation is faulty. The cracks on your wall just reflect that deeper problem."

"I'm listening. Go on," I replied, interested to get to the bottom of this.

don't fix your foundation, you will forever be patchwork on your walls. You don't need a painter first. You need someone to work on your foundation. When that is done, I'll fix the cracks."

He was right. I got the foundation fixed, he patched up the cracks, and they haven't been back since.

The cracks I experienced on the wall of my home are a perfect visual image for the condition of our nation today. We can see "cracks" everywhere: social cracks, financial cracks, racial cracks, political cracks, moral cracks, even crack-cocaine cracks. But until we stabilize the foundation, no number of programs, government grants, or elections will be able to repair the cracks in our cultural walls. We have already spent a great deal of time, money, and energy trying to patch up these problems, but the real cause is our foundation, so the problems just keeping coming back and with a vengeance.

Solid or Shaky Foundation?

In Matthew 7, toward the end of His Sermon on the Mount, Jesus told a similar story about the need for a solid foundation. In this telling, we read about two very different men who were each building a house. Same supplies. Same goal. Yet two very different foundations.

One man built his house on the shaky and uncertain

foundation of sand. The other man built his house on the solid foundation of rock. The test of these foundations happened quickly when the storms hit. The winds raged and the rains fell, beating against these two houses. The foundation that had been built upon the sand quickly crumbled, while the house on the strong foundation remained intact (Matthew 7:24-27).

In this parable, the rock referred to the man who heard the Word of God and applied it. The sand referred to the man who also heard the Word of God, but did *not* apply it.

This parable represents anything we build either with wisdom (hearing and applying the Word of God) or foolishly (without applying the Word of God). In the Bible, a house can represent a number of things: a life, family, a church, and even a nation (such as the house of Israel).

Thus, if and when we seek to build our nation on anything other than the stable foundation of the wisdom of God, what we build will not last when life's trials and challenges come upon us. Rather, we will spend all of our time and money focusing on the fissures.

Wisdom is our capacity to apply spiritual truth to life's realities. Foolishness in the Bible has nothing to do with degrees or education; it has to do with the inability or refusal to apply spiritual truths to our choices. It was the application of what was heard that determined the foundation of rock, not the information itself that determined the foundation. Both men heard the same thing. Only one applied it. This is why people can sit in church, or read books, or listen to sermons online and be adequately informed, yet never be transformed. Because they have the information without the application. A solid foundation is built on the application of God's Word.

> *A solid foundation is built on the application of God's Word.*

Foundations are always where you start when building. Everything else depends on how solid the foundation is of a building, a life, a home, a ministry, or even of a nation. Foundations on rock are very hard to construct because they require drilling. The process takes time, effort. Foundations on rock won't happen overnight. But foundations on sand are pretty quick.

But to take your time with the foundation is absolutely critical depending on the kind of structure you want to build. Doors are important, windows are important, roofs are important, but foundations are essential. Because when that foundation is inferior, nothing else matters.

When someone builds a skyscraper in the midst of a city, you can always know how high builders want to go up by looking at how deep they drill down. The higher the skyscraper, the deeper the pit into which to pour the foundation. You can't build a skyscraper on the foundation of a chicken coop. Neither can you build a strong nation on such a foundation. Like sand castles on the shore of a rising tide, our country and our culture are quickly being washed away.

Kingdom Citizens and Kingdom Churches

If America is going to rebuild itself morally, socially, and spiritually, it is going to have to begin by fortifying the foundation.

But how does America do that?

Through each one of us functioning as a kingdom citizen.

We must focus on fortifying our own foundations first because the health of a nation reflects the health of its citizens. Strong citizens comprise a strong nation. You and I cannot be responsible for everyone else, but we are responsible for ourselves as well as the people we can influence.

Each member of the body of Christ, as well as the collective church, must begin reflecting at a higher level the foundational values of the Kingdom of God. Yet we can't do that unless and until we understand and apply the principles and precepts of God's Word.

Our society is crumbling today because we have dug up and replaced our once-firm foundation with sand. In our own focus on expansion, too often the church has ended up settling for buildings and programs instead of advancing the Kingdom of God on earth.

We've had church, but we haven't had transformation.

Unless the church becomes kingdom minded, we are not being the church Christ came to build. Few people are aware that Jesus mentioned "church" only three times in His earthly ministry—and all three times are recorded in the kingdom-focused book of Matthew. This same book of Matthew uses the word "kingdom" fifty-four times.

We've had church, but we haven't had transformation.

Yet which do we hear more about—churches or the Kingdom? Instead of seeking to promote the Kingdom, we have focused on planting churches. Our seminaries teach our future spiritual leaders how to grow churches rather than how to advance the Kingdom.

I'm not saying to get rid of church—I'm a pastor of one, so of course that's not my point. But I am saying we ought to focus on *both* the Kingdom and the church because both are linked. We can't have church without the Kingdom, while the Kingdom carries out its agenda through the church.

It is high time we become kingdom people as a church, representing something bigger than our own personalities, programs, and platforms. We need to make God's Kingdom our rule and His glory our goal. God didn't establish the church to make us feel good; He established it to prevail against the gates of hell through developing kingdom disciples.

The heart of our problem today is not new. It is an age-old problem that shows up when religion rules over relationship. It shows up when ease overcomes zeal. It showed up in Sodom and Gomorrah shortly before their destruction. And it showed up in 2 Chronicles 15 when Israel faced disturbances, afflictions, wars, internal chaos, and more. Scripture says:

> For many days Israel was without the true God and without a teaching priest and without law. . . . In those times there was no peace to him who went out or to him who came in, for many disturbances afflicted all the inhabitants of the lands. Nation was crushed by nation, and city by city, for God troubled them with every kind of distress. (2 Chronicles 15:3, 5-6)

We can see through this passage that people could not go to their houses without conflict; they couldn't even go out without conflict. They couldn't go to work without conflict or live within their communities without conflict. All the inhabitants of the land had become engulfed in this lack of harmony and stability in the culture.

The passage goes on to say that nation was crushed by nation and city by city. Sound familiar? Reminds me of what our evening news is about every single day—in Chicago, Baltimore, Saint Paul, Dallas, Baton Rouge, or name any city at all. It doesn't seem to matter anymore where you live. Whether it's racial conflict on the rise again, or class conflict between Wall Street and the 99-percenters, or immigration conflict, terrorism, the threat of ISIS—we have conflict.

Israel faced these things as well. There was urban conflict (city by city). There was national conflict (nation by nation). So the question comes up: Why all of this conflict?

Essentially God said, "See that mess? Blame it on Me."

Now, I would have thought that with all of this chaos, the biblical text would have read, "for the devil troubled them with every kind of distress." I would have thought when you have this much hell on earth, this much disruption in society, this much madness on individual, familial, communal, and international levels, Satan would be directly blamed. But the passage says something very different. It says something that might totally surprise you. It surprised me when I first read it. It says, "God troubled them with every kind of distress."

God troubled them. Essentially God said, "See that mess? Blame it on Me."

What I would like to suggest to you, based on this passage, is a complete paradigm shift from the ways we have been viewing issues in our culture for decades. What I would like to suggest from this text most likely differs from your worldview. But what I would like to suggest to you is that what you and I are watching on the news—on television or through whatever means we get our information about the deterioration and the devolution of our nation—is actually the passive wrath of God, broadcast to us in "high definition."

The Wrath of God

What do I mean? We are all familiar with the active wrath of God. That is when fire and brimstone fall directly from heaven at His command. Sodom and Gomorrah represent the perfect example. This is where God actively commands His surrogates, His angels, to bring about destruction at His command. The active wrath of God is the normative method of discipline in the Old Testament. Yet with the death and resurrection of Jesus Christ, God's relationship to the world shifted. According to 2 Corinthians 5:19-21, God reconciled the world to Himself. Verse 21 says, "He made Him who knew no sin to be sin on our behalf, so that we might become the righteousness of God in Him." With this shift, fire and brimstone no longer normatively fell from heaven as it did in the previous dispensation. The death of Jesus Christ ushered in a new season by rerouting God's wrath.

God now predominantly expresses His anger toward sin (because He hasn't changed His nature toward sin) in a passive way. The first chapter of Romans describes this for us in depth. We are introduced to it in verse 18, "For the wrath of God is revealed from heaven against all ungodliness and unrighteousness of men who suppress the truth in unrighteousness." Three times throughout the next several verses God reveals how this wrath is carried out. We read:

> Therefore *God gave them over.* (verse 24)
> For this reason *God gave them over.* (verse 26)
> And just as they did not see fit to acknowledge God any longer, *God gave them over.* (verse 28)

God gave them over. God released them to life without Him. To paraphrase, God said, "Since you do not want Me, I will let you know what it looks like when you do not have Me. I release you to your independence from Me."

As a result of hearts hardening toward and turning from Him, God allows—as the natural consequence of spiritual rebellion—internal damage and deterioration to occur and then spread. It's not that the people referenced in Romans didn't know God either. In fact we read, "For even though they knew God, they did not honor Him as God or give thanks" (verse 21). They knew God, yes. They had just decided to distance themselves from God and His Word by suppressing "the truth in unrighteousness." This distance is the same distance we see in the Old Testament times of spiritual judgment—the distance serving as the core cause of those judgments.

While the methods may not line up identically between the Old Covenant dispensation and the New, the root of individual, family, and societal mess still stems from the same cause—distance from God.

The problem with our country today is not that God is not near. The problem is that we, the people, turn too quickly between near and far. We turn too quickly between God and other things that we look to in His place. As a result, the United States of America is undergoing the consequences of distance from God. We have removed ourselves from close proximity to Him and are paying a hefty social, political, familial, and economic cost for doing so.

Our nation's ills are not merely the result of corrupt politicians, terrorists, or extremists. Our troubles can be traced directly to ineffective Christians. The tragedy today is not that sinners sin; that's what they're expected to do, since mankind is born in sin and shaped in iniquity (Psalm 51:5; Ephesians 2:1-3). The real tragedy is that the church as a whole has failed to advance God's Kingdom and principles in society in order to be a positive influence for good in our nation and in our world.

God has been asked to exit a culture that has uninvited and "unfriended" Him. Therefore, He has given us over to all that results from living independently of Him. Within the very sin itself comes wrapped the passive wrath of God.

When God Is the Problem

We witness a similar situation in Joel 2. The scene is set with the telling of a great disaster falling upon Israel. Armies invaded. The land trembled. People were in anguish. The earth quaked. And locusts swarmed.

Yet all of this destruction happened for a reason. The terror, loss, and locust invasion were not merely natural phenomena. Rather, this all happened because God wanted to make a spiritual point. Joel 2:25 tells us clearly that God Himself caused these swarms of locusts along with other forces of destruction. They were "My great army which I sent among you."

Because the people didn't quite catch that point, God sent His prophet Joel to help them understand what was happening. They weren't connecting the dots on their own. And what happened back then happens today. We, the people of God, far too often fail to make the connection between what appears to be a natural phenomenon and what really is God's supernatural intentionality.

Turn on the evening news or political talk shows at any given time and you will be privy to turmoil and ruin of all measures. True, some stories rise to the surface as having a greater and more long-term impact, but the sheer volume of crises in our land today is alarming. Yet, despite it all,

What happened back then happens today.

we rarely make any spiritual connection to any of it. We just think that the housing mortgage industry failed, the economy tanked, the collective health of our citizenry has diminished, families simply were redefined, and prisons somehow became too full, while government likewise grew too large.

We block out the repercussions of what insurance companies not-so-ironically call "acts of God." Maybe it's just a storm here or a disaster there. Then another one, and another one again. All the while, we ignore the sound of trees being harvested for the paper on which is printed that ever-growing disaster "bill." Since 1980, we've had over 150 of these "acts of God"—weather or climate devastations—racking up a bill of more than four trillion dollars. No typo there, that's a "T" for trillion, as in "tragic."

As we see in this example from the book of Joel, God

sent His army of destruction to wake up His people, not to judge the rest of the world.

God was Israel's problem.

God summoned the locusts.

God sent the storms.

God opened the front lines for their enemies to advance.

God was the aggressor—not the Hittites, Philistines, or any other "ites" or "ines."

Just God.

And when God is your problem, only God is your solution.

Our symptoms today—physical, social, financial, racial issues, and more—are merely the fruit. Which is why we will never achieve lasting solutions until we—members of Christ's body—fiercely return to God and reflect that return in our impact and influence on the culture as kingdom citizens. Until we hear His heart. Until we fast and pray, for days. Until we become unified and seek His face.

The solutions to our nation's problems will not first and foremost be found in the White House. Our solutions will first be found in God's house because He is ultimately in charge and His people have priority access to Him.

If God is our problem, then it doesn't really matter who we elect. If God is the source of our cultural chaos, it doesn't really matter what programs we put into place. Because if God is the One who is ticked off, then He is the

One bringing about the disintegration and disorder in our culture.

Three Things Gone Missing

Tucked within the trenches of 2 Chronicles 15 is the revelation of three crucial components that can trigger God's wrath. Before we are introduced to the chaos in verse 5, we are given its cause: "And for many days Israel was without the true God and without a teaching priest and without law."

Three things had gone missing in the culture:

- The true God
- The teaching priests
- God's law and principles

In the historical recording, the chronicler was not saying that the Israelites had become atheists or no longer believed in God. He was not saying there weren't theological discussions occurring. The sacrificial fires at the temple were still going. Israel had religion in full force. But Israel had lost a correct relationship with God. The nation was no longer functioning according to His covenantal standards.

A Kingdom Without a King

The Israelites wanted a convenient God, one they could control. They wanted a kingdom without a King. They wanted a figurehead with the trappings of kingship only. Yet any god, or king, you can boss around isn't the true God or King. The true God does not adjust to you. You adjust to Him.

Similarly, most people in the U.S. do not want the true God interfering with their lives either, or reminding us that He has an agenda greater than our own. Our culture wants to pay homage only—to offer a nice little prayer before public meetings, maybe even a parade. Or we're content with a nice little service before our sports games on Sunday or before we take our naps or have our dinners and go to a movie.

We are reinforcing our culture's false view of God.

But any time we simply pay homage without aligning our thoughts and actions under God, we are reinforcing our culture's false view of God. We are framing Him as a harmless deity with nothing significant to say about the educational, scientific, entertainment, civic, political, familial, legal, or racial issues of the day. Doing so, we seek to leave God the title of King in name only, and give His powers and authority to others, or even claim them for ourselves.

All throughout the Old Testament, we witness the constant battle between the true God and false gods (idols). Idolatry is any noun (person, place, thing, or idea) that is looked to as a defining factor or source. Idols in Scripture were not just things that people worshiped. They were things people looked to in order to gain benefit from them.

Ba'al wasn't worshiped just for the sake of worship. Ba'al was worshiped with the hope that the god would fertilize a man's property (land or wives) and cause it to bear fruit. False gods like Ba'al were believed to provide a benefit to their followers.

This may surprise you, but idols come in all shapes and sizes. Idols are not merely statues made of wood or figurines carved in some far-off country. You can make an idol of the American flag when you wrap civil religion in it and allow it to usurp the Kingdom of God. Whenever you put America and God on equal footing, you have now created a false god called civil religion.

You can make an idol of your race. Whenever black is not biblical and white does not agree with holy writ, then what you are doing is compromising God and encasing the God of the Bible in your color, culture, class, background, or history. Any time God is diminished and you look to find your identity, values, or beliefs outside of God, you have become an idolater. Your career can be an idol. Your need to buy more things—more clothes, more trinkets, more toys—in order to satisfy yourself and define your existence, can be an idol. Politics can be an idol. If and when you are more Republican or more Democrat than you are Christian, you have placed yourself under a false god.

Israel had allowed politics to interfere with God's house. God had made it clear that His house was to have only one throne—His own. But Israel brought its own kings into the temple. Because of that, God's glory left. God's covering departed. God's influence, power, protection, and guidance were removed because Israel placed another throne next to His own. Ezekiel 43:7-9 reads:

> He [God] said to me, "Son of man, this is the place of My throne and the place of the soles of My feet, where I will dwell among the sons of Israel forever. And the house of Israel will not again defile My holy name, neither they nor their kings, by their harlotry and by the corpses of their kings when they die, by setting their threshold by My threshold and their door post beside My door post, with only the wall between Me and them. And they have defiled My holy name by their abominations which they have committed. So I have consumed them in My anger. Now let them put away their harlotry and the corpses of their kings far from Me; and I will dwell among them forever."

In my Evans translation, it goes like this:

> This is My holy temple. Do not bring the thrones of your kings and sit them next to My throne. Do not

bring your politicians and policies and sit them next to Me as if I ride the backs of donkeys or elephants. Do not bring your governors and leaders and put them next to Me and think we are equal and on the same page. We are not equal. We are not on the same page. Separate My throne from their thrones because it is not the same throne.

God created the church to act as a vehicle for His rule, laws, and glory. It is not the Democrats' view and God's view that we are to proclaim in the church. Neither is it the Republicans' view and God's view that we are to possess. It is not their rule and God's rule in His house. It is only God who rules.

Yet far too many churches have been corrupted by civil religion. They have failed to distinguish the difference between partisan politics and God's Kingdom. This plays out in more areas than simply politics, though. It plays out in bringing the world's values into God's house and raising them up to receive the same level of adherence and attention as God, if not more. This has resulted in many Christians becoming citizens of the culture rather than citizens of the Kingdom.

Because the church has lost its own conscience in many ways, it has failed in its calling to be a conscience for society—not only through the civic participation of its members, but also through their own daily governance in their personal lives and families. We have allowed what society provides in our media, music, schools, policies, and philosophies to infiltrate and infect the church.

We have made our very own culture an idol while putting the God of the universe on the discount rack. We want God on the loop—existing outside of the center point of our lives, rather than in the midst of them. We are behaving like the Israelites in many ways who wanted a god they could control, a god to whom they could dictate, a god they could boss or appease. The people of Israel had replaced the true God with their own idols. But that was not the only problem.

Teachers Without the Truth

The second problem in Israel was the lack of teaching priests. Again, the historical recording doesn't say there were no priests, just that the priests had stopped teaching the truth. There were plenty of priests at that time. It's just that they had traded truth for tradition. Worship and preaching had degenerated into an activity for selfish gain and promotion.

Sound familiar?

Too often in our nation, pastors preach to please. Each fears that someone might say, "Well, I didn't like that sermon." We worry more about filling the pews than speaking the truth. The real issue is whether what we teach is true, not whether it is popular. Politicians need to be popular. Preachers need to tell the truth.

The issue of truth is all-important. The lack of truth leads to a "conscienceless" society. People become anesthetized in their consciences, losing their sense of right and wrong. In such a society, every person becomes a law unto himself, so chaos rules.

We are suffering today from a case of spiritual AIDS. Physical AIDS is a breakdown of the immune system due to a virus. When the virus attacks, it attacks the immune system. Our immune system is set up to ward off bacteria and other things that would seek to do us in. Because of our immune system, colds don't usually turn into pneumonia. We fight off cancer regularly. But when the immune system is down, watch out. Viruses and bacteria produce all kinds of diseases. Even death.

We, the church, are supposed to be the immune system to the world.

What the church is doing today is looking at the world and saying, "Look at all the evil viruses and bacteria out there—that's terrible!" But wait a minute before you judge so quickly because we, the church, are supposed to be the immune system to the world. We are the salt to preserve the culture and the light. We are to drive out the darkness

(Matthew 5:13-16). Remember, one of the reasons Sodom and Gomorrah were judged was because the righteous couldn't be located (Genesis 19:22-33).

The bacteria of evil has proliferated in America as it has because the immune system called the church is compromised. Thus, cultural colds have degenerated into societal pneumonia. When preachers and teachers no longer teach truth in love, there is no standard of rightness anymore.

A Society Without Restraints

When the absolute standard of God's Word is dismissed or "dumbed down," this leads to the third missing component in Israel's culture—God's law. When a culture has a false view of God built on bad information, God begins to remove the restraint of His law, and evil grows unbridled. What you and I are witnessing today in the rapid deterioration of our culture is the reality that God is removing more and more of His restraint.

Even sinners who respect God won't do certain things. But once God is removed from or marginalized in a culture, then the standard for a society is gone and God Himself becomes one's worst nightmare. When God leaves a society, hope goes with Him. Just as people and their taxes leave the city and go to the suburbs, when God is removed, He goes to the spiritual suburbs and the city's culture deteriorates.

In other words, postmodernism sets in. Postmodernism simply states that there are no overriding absolutes to govern everything. Essentially, we all get to make up our own rules. And because truth has gotten dumbed down in the church, it has gotten dumbed down in society. People become a law unto themselves, resulting in cultural chaos.

We replicate the disintegration that took place in Israel when every person did what was right in his or her own eyes (Judges 21:25). The problem of gun violence in our cities is not just about guns. The greater problem is people without a conscience having guns. When you lack a properly informed conscience because there is no longer equity, justice, or a common law, there are no standards to regulate you anymore.

When I walk through airport security checkpoints that have magnetometers, the machine beeps if I have keys in my pocket. I have to go back and take my keys out of my pocket in order to go through it without beeping. Yet there have been times when I have walked through with keys in my pocket and it didn't beep. Why? Because those magnetometers have to be set. The person who sets them and the level of sensitivity they are set to determine what triggers them.

We have generations of citizens in our culture today whose consciences no longer "beep." It is not just the young people—it's our teaching priests, the members of our churches, and we who call ourselves believers in Christ. We have allowed the world to set our conscience rather than the Word. Thus, there are no standards in school, no standards in the home, and no standards on television, social media, and the like. Yes, we'll complain, but we'll also watch it, sing it, post it—and advertise it.

In 2 Chronicles 15:6, God was the cause of Israel's distress, not the sinners in that culture and not even Satan. Read it one more time: "God troubled them with every kind of distress."

God troubled them.

Friend, when God is your problem, only God is your solution.

If God is upset, it doesn't matter who we elect or what programs we initiate. Until His anger is assuaged, we won't be able to fix what's wrong or spend enough money to buy our way out of our dilemmas.

What He says must overrule what we say or think.

This is the heart of our problem today. We have marginalized God. And as long as we keep God at a distance, He will not take over the "control center" of our world, and thus unrighteousness will rule and wreak havoc.

We hold within the collective body of Christ not only the power but also the capacity to put our country back on the path of ascendancy. How? By returning to the One True God and aligning our time, thoughts, talents, and treasures under Him (verse 4).

What He says must overrule what we say or think.

What He says must surpass our own human politics, secular social movements, and religious traditions. What He says must prevail over our own personal choices.

It is time we recognize that the Kingdom of God is not some ethereal fairy tale located in some far-off land. The Kingdom of God is here, and it is now.

And we have offended its King.

2

SELFIES OR SERVICE

Maged Shahata had been born into poverty, as were his three children. A follower of Jesus in a nation of Islam, Maged had little hope or opportunity for a future brighter than his past. Living as part of a religious minority in a nation that is at least 90 percent Islamic came with its own challenges, including discrimination and oppression.

Maged longed for a better life for his children. Because of this, he chose to take a risk. He hoped to get better pay by finding employment in an Islamic nation more extremist than his own. Maged's risk enabled his eldest daughter to enter college, something no one in his family had ever accomplished.

Hani Messihah, another Christian, also loved his four children—three boys and a girl. His devoted wife, Magda, adored Hani's laughter in their home and often remarked how kind he was, that he was given to sharing hugs and kisses at will. She called him her angel.

Hani was always good for telling a joke or bringing a smile to someone's face. But he was also a dedicated and responsible family man. Wanting to provide for his wife and children at a level he could never reach in his own country, he moved to another land to give his family the daily food and shelter they needed. Hani knew this new country came with great risk due to his faith, but he was willing to take that risk so his children could have enough to eat and attend a good school.

Yousef Shoukry was a quiet, 24-year-old man said to have the pure heart of a child. He dreamed of one day getting married and starting his own family. A believer in Jesus Christ from an impoverished town in Egypt, Yousef knew he had to venture elsewhere to make enough money for that dream to come true. So Yousef decided to move to Libya and seek employment there.

Kingdom man after kingdom man refused to recant.

His mother begged him not to go, knowing the dangers a Christian faced in Libya. But Yousef knew he had no choice but to work there. He needed the income to one day offer his own children an opportunity to avoid becoming stuck, like he had been, in Egypt's oppressive, impoverished environment.

Maged, Hani, and Yousef were men of great courage. These men were kingdom men. They sought to better their families' lives through their own personal sacrifice. Yet in the process, they were tested by an ideology that cost them their lives.

On February 15, 2015, Maged, Hani, Yousef, and eighteen others knelt as captives on a beach along the southern Mediterranean coast in Libya.[1] Their captors, Islamic extremists, called them "people of the cross." That was the nature of their crime. Twenty of the twenty-one men would later be confirmed as Egyptian Coptic Christians. The twenty-first man was not a Christian or an Egyptian at all. Sources say he was from Chad or Ghana, and his name was Matthew Ayairga.

As the Islamic extremists went down the row wielding a tool to cut off the heads of the kneeling believers, each was commanded to recant of his faith and claim loyalty to Allah in order to save his life. Kingdom man after kingdom man refused to recant, most mumbling the words *Ya Rabbi Yasou* (O My Lord Jesus) instead. Thus, kingdom man after kingdom man lost his life.

The twenty-first man, who was not a Coptic Christian, was also told to pledge allegiance to Allah, the god of Islam. What is reported next ought to do more than send chills up your spine and bring a sigh of amazement from your mouth, as it did mine. What happened next ought to challenge us to reexamine our own lives and the level of our own faith.

It was reported that because Ayairga had witnessed the

immense faith and commitment of the twenty other men, when it came time for him to pledge allegiance to Allah, he looked down the line and then back up to his captors, stating, "Their God is my God." Ayairga spoke this knowing that doing so would cost him everything.

Yet he spoke it boldly, "Their God is my God."[2]

A Faith Worth Dying For?

The words haunt me even as I write this chapter. This man had witnessed such powerful faith, dedication, and commitment in the lives of his fellow prisoners that he converted to Christ at the expense of his very own life. Whatever faith these other men had that allowed them to leave life with such strong, committed dignity and hope was a faith, and a God, Ayairga could believe in.

I write that the words haunt me because as I look at our nation today, at those of us who call ourselves "followers of Jesus" and "people of the cross," I wonder: Would anyone be willing to give up his or her life in order to be saved because of witnessing our own commitment to *Ya Rabbi Yasou*? Would anyone see our lives and say in the face of imminent death, "Their God is my God"?

I wonder.

Or, rather, do those outside the church look at the contemporary church of Jesus in America today and find little more than a religious social club? It is comprised of people no different from the society we've been called to transform.

Of the nearly 60 million abortions performed since Roe v. Wade, over half have been performed on women of "faith."[3] While the statistics on divorce are debatable based on whose study you read, few pastors will debate the reality that divorce happens at an alarming rate in our churches, as does spousal abuse, both physical and emotional. Similarly, pornography has laid claim to our men by the droves. Our entertainment and our music frequently look no different from the world's. And less culturally obvious sins (but just as severe in God's eyes) such as materialism, greed, and gluttony ravage both our bodies and our billfolds. Those displays often receive the "likes" on social media in place of acts of service and love.[4]

> *What do you call fruit that begins to eat itself? Rotten.*

Is anyone seeing our lives, our sacrifices, and our dedication and saying, "Their God is my God"?

We have only to look at the indicators within our own four walls and underneath our own steeples to recognize that far too many individuals, families, and churches are simply cannibalizing into self-destruction. We have been called to bear fruit. But what do you call fruit that begins to eat itself? Rotten. Because of this, our society is overrun by the enemy's agenda of chaos and upheaval.

Few, if any, say "Their God is my God" because few, if any, witness radical life change, commitment, and sacrificial service to the glory of God. The narcissism that runs rampant through our culture's veins flows freely on the streams of our own social sites as well.

So why should we be surprised that a nation comprised of roughly 71 percent of those claiming some form of faith in the God of the Bible (as our nation is) has little or no positive impact on our society?[5]

Because 71 percent of anything *should have* an impact.

Yet a cursory glance around our country leads me to wonder if we are leaving any mark at all—outside of our own buildings, that is, which are complete with lattes before church services and, for most, sitting empty the rest of the week.

If you are not convinced and need more facts to be convinced of the anemic impact we have on our nation, consider these statistics from a recent study.[6] When asked what impact the Christian faith has on our culture, the following percentages reflect those who said it has either no impact at all or a negative impact on these areas:

- 62 percent said none/or negative on differences of opinion being discussed in a civil manner
- 66 percent said none/or negative on ethics in the business world
- 67 percent said none/or negative on participation in politics or voting

- 67 percent said none/or negative on the amount of racism in society
- 69 percent said none/or negative on how people treat the environment
- 73 percent said none/or negative on how the US is viewed by other nations

When reducing that sampling to only those who claim to attend church, 52 percent of church attendees said the Christian faith has either no impact, or even a negative impact, on our society as a whole.

As a result, the church today, and we who comprise it, are all too often ridiculed, criticized, rejected outright, or simply ignored in the public arena. We often blame this on others—the secular media or special interest groups. But do we deserve any of that blame ourselves? Somehow, while managing to raise enough money to build more churches and produce more members than ever before, we have become only more ineffective in our efforts to influence our culture for Christ at the deepest foundational levels.

> *Do we deserve any of that blame ourselves?*

The truth of the matter is, too often the church has failed to develop disciples of Jesus Christ who effectively function as kingdom citizens in the culture. Many churches have made membership the goal at the expense of discipleship, thus failing to clearly demonstrate the solutions of the Kingdom for the critical issues of our day. We are no longer "salt" in a decaying culture (Matthew 5:13). Yes, we continue to do an admirable job of cursing the darkness. But we have done a poor job of spreading the light (Matthew 5:14-16).

As a result, our national security is threatened, our government has become ineffectively overgrown, we are facing a looming health-care crisis, marriage has been redefined, gender has been redefined, races are in conflict, terrorists have bombed public places, children succumb to educational disparity and gender confusion, we are unfairly represented in taxation, public safety is an elusive right, and our elections have become the laughingstock of our world.

Our society has declined economically, materially, and educationally.

Our criminal justice system cannot begin to handle the increase in crime that keeps the general urban population living behind barred windows and doors while gangs, criminals, and drug dealers control the streets. Prisons can't be built fast enough to house the number of criminals the system seeks to incarcerate.

Nor has increased educational funding stemmed the tide of moral decay now engulfing us. Metal detectors are now common at many high schools. Condoms are distributed for free.

Numerous books, seminars, workshops, and symposia have not enabled us to bridge the philosophical and ethical divides that separate us. Our technological advances have far outpaced our sense of personal and national responsibility. We can send a robotic probe to examine the surface of Mars, but we cannot manage to pay our bills, or wisely choose which costs to incur as a nation. As a result, our society has declined economically, materially, and educationally. We are one of the world's wealthiest nations, yet all the while, we are made up of the world's most obese and unhealthy citizens, even our children.

The Mind-set of a Kingdom Citizen

As I mentioned before, a kingdom citizen is *a visible, verbal follower of Jesus Christ who consistently applies the principles of heaven to the concerns of the culture.* Yet it is difficult to be a kingdom citizen without a proper understanding of the Kingdom. Unfortunately today, far too few fully understand God's Kingdom. Without an understanding of the Kingdom, it is impossible to prevail over much of anything. It is also impossible to fully embody what it means to live as a kingdom citizen.

If you are an American, you are most likely an American because you were born here. If you are a kingdom citizen, it is because you have been born again into God's

Kingdom (Colossians 1:13). You do not want to miss fully comprehending the Kingdom because it not only affects you, but also because it is the key to understanding the Word of God. The unifying central theme throughout Scripture is the glory of God and the advancement of His Kingdom. The conjoining thread from Genesis to Revelation—from beginning to end—focuses on one thing: God's glory through advancing God's Kingdom.

When you are unaware of that theme, the Bible exists as disconnected stories that are great for inspiration but seem to be unrelated in purpose and direction. Scripture exists to share God's movement in history toward the establishment and expansion of His Kingdom. Understanding that concept increases the relevancy of this several-thousand-year-old manuscript to your day-to-day living.

Throughout the Bible, the Kingdom of God is His rule, His plan, His program. God's Kingdom is all-embracing. It covers everything in the universe. In fact, we can define the Kingdom as God's comprehensive rule over all creation. It is the rule of God (theocracy) and not the rule of man (homocracy) that reigns paramount.

Now if God's Kingdom is comprehensive, so is His kingdom agenda. The kingdom agenda, then, may be defined as *the visible manifestation of the comprehensive rule of God over every area of life.*

The reason so many of us as individuals, and collectively as the church, are not having a greater impact on our nation is that we have lost sight of God's kingdom agenda. We want God to okay our plans rather than wanting to fulfill His plans. We want God to bring us glory rather than wanting to bring Him glory. We want "my kingdom come," not "Thy kingdom come."

In many ways we want God, or at least His rule, sidelined.

Now, before you go and point a haughty finger, thinking that statement is about someone else—those people who removed prayer from schools, those people who have allowed transgender bathrooms, those people who have _____ (fill in the blank with whatever you want)—bear in mind that God (His principles, rule, kingdom priorities, and agenda) has similarly been removed from many churches as well. We have more churches now than ever before. We have larger churches now than ever before. But we have less of God's presence, power, and authority than ever before.

We, His body, have become too proud to prioritize Him as a way of life and make Him a focal point of our existence. We have become too self-absorbed to make sacrifices equating to much more than a meal for a homeless man, as we sip our five-dollar coffee in our car and post our "good deed" on our social media sites for all to see.

We have become far more fascinated with selfies than service.

We complain that prayer and Scripture have been removed from public places, but how many of our preachers today preach the Word of God? Many, if not most, offer up instead a 17-minute motivational talk quoting from popular authors. A mist in the pulpit is always a fog in the pew. In other words, a lack of clarity among the clergy leads to chaos in the culture.

As a result, we have not only become a valueless society but also a church without impact. Cracks exist not only in our culture but also in our congregations. We have forgotten that the church does not exist for the church. The moment the church exists for the church, it is no longer being the church.

> *God created the church for the benefit of the Kingdom.*

God created the church for the benefit of the Kingdom. For His purposes. He established the church to give us the keys to a whole other realm. He didn't place us here to be popular. Like referees in a football game, we won't make decisions that everyone likes. Sometimes the crowd will jeer at us, but that's okay. We don't work for them. We serve a King from another Kingdom who rules with supreme authority. And as His kingdom citizens, we have full access to this authority.

Speaking to the church, Jesus in Matthew 16:19 tells us, "I will give you the keys of the kingdom of heaven;

and whatever you bind on earth shall have been bound in heaven, and whatever you loose on earth shall have been loosed in heaven."

What do you do with keys? You gain access (see Isaiah 22:22). Have you ever been in a hurry and you couldn't find your keys? That means that you're not going anywhere anytime soon. Or perhaps you are like me, and you have a number of keys on your key chain, but you have forgotten what some of them unlock. Those keys are no longer of any benefit to you.

Jesus says the kingdom-minded church that develops kingdom disciples resulting in kingdom-minded citizens will have the keys to the Kingdom of God, giving it the authority to bind and loose on earth and in heaven. Yet why are we not experiencing this power and authority as kingdom citizens today? Because we are not building on a kingdom-minded foundation. We are building on the sands of "churchdom" instead. Therefore, we are trying to use our own church "keys" to unlock kingdom "doors," and finding that they don't open much of anything at all.

When we as individuals, and our churches, are not kingdom minded—when we fail to comprehend, let alone adopt, a kingdom theology, ideology, and methodology—we are unable to open heaven's doors. Yes, we have prayer meetings, preaching, choir songs, and seminars, but we also have no authority. We have no authority because the authority is directly tied to the Kingdom. The keys of the Kingdom don't belong to buildings; they belong to the King.

If we could ever see the Kingdom as God sees it, and if we could ever view each other as God views us—designed to come together in a unified goal underneath His overarching agenda—then the world would have to deal with the strength of the church of Jesus Christ. Right now the world merely needs to deal with this segment over here, and that segment over there, as we divide ourselves over platforms and preferences.

This is not to negate or downplay the great work countless churches have done throughout time in our land. I applaud and am grateful for all of it. What we have been ineffective at is a unity that increases our impact on a larger collective level. When we unite, as so many churches did during the civil rights movement, we can bring hope and healing where as a nation we need it most.

If Hell Is in the Pew

People frequently view churches today as places to congregate. Church is a place to find encouragement, inspiration, and friendship. And while those things are both good and important, when we make them our entire focus we alter the meaning of church. When Jesus spoke of the church,

He spoke of a spiritual legislative body. This was a group of people who had been tasked to enact heaven's viewpoint in the midst of a hellish society. This *ecclesia* (the term used for church) was comprised of people called out to govern for God by applying relevant spiritual truth to the matters of man.

In Greek societies, if you were a part of the ecclesia, you were part of the governing council. You legislated on behalf of the Greek population (see Acts 19:38-41). Ecclesia wasn't a location at which to socialize. It wasn't a place to come sing a song or hear a sermon. Ecclesia was the location of legislation.

> *The biblical church exists to advance the Kingdom, not simply to defend it.*

This legislative function of the church is clearly evident in Jesus' words. Jesus specifically references the "gates of hell." "Gates" are used in Scripture to refer to a place where legislative activities occur (Zechariah 8:16; Deuteronomy 16:18). Reinforcing this reality is the fact that "keys" gain access to heaven's authority. This is the same authority that will then be carried out by the church on earth (Matthew 16:19). Jesus sits at the right hand of the Father to legislate from heaven, and we sit with Him (Ephesians 2:5-6).

The church is not merely a place for spiritual inspiration or information. The church exists as the place where the values of eternity operate in history so that history sees what God looks like when heaven is operating on earth. The job of the church is not to adopt the culture, or to merely assess and analyze the culture, but, through its kingdom citizens, to set heaven within the context of culture so that the culture can see God at work in the midst of the conflicts of men.

The biblical church exists to advance the Kingdom, not simply to defend it. In speaking about the foundation of the church, Jesus said, "Upon this rock I will build My church; and the gates of Hades will not overpower it" (Matthew 16:18).

Jesus said He would build His church on the foundation of a rock.

However, for far too long the gates of hades have overpowered the church. The church has been reacting to the movements of hell rather than setting the pace of heaven. Jesus clearly says that the way you will know that the church is His church is that hell will be trying to stop it, and hell will fail. It's as simple as that.

Hell will fail.

Yet when the church is not unified as one, a rock, the reverse will occur, because that is the way Christ has designed the church to function. Without oneness, the gates of hades—Satan and his minions—will overpower and engulf us.

This truth reminds me of when Hurricane Katrina

struck the US Gulf Coast. Hurricane Katrina was bad, but she wasn't the ultimate problem. Katrina had blown in, done her thing, and she was on her way. The ultimate trouble didn't come from Katrina; rather it came when the levee broke. That's when the city flooded.

The levee existed to hold back the water. Had the levee held, Katrina would have been remembered as just another strong storm in a long line of others, rather than as the disaster that she birthed.

God has placed a levee in history. It is us, His church. We exist as a spiritual legislative body to hold back Satan's forces from being unleashed against mankind. The church isn't solely about choir fests, programs, and luncheons. The church isn't just about feeling something, praying, clapping, singing, or saying "amen."

The church was intentionally designed so that the strongest forces cannot break it down. The gates of hell will not overpower it.

But if hell is on the doorstep, in the lobby, or in the pew of the church in the United States—which many would argue is true—this can only be the result of the body of Christ failing to join together as a unified whole in pursuit of a kingdom agenda.

We know this is true because Jesus made it clear that He would build His church in such a way that, when done His way, the gates of hell would not prevail.

3

A Servant,
Not a System

Whenever you lose your ability to affect the culture around you for good, the society as a whole loses a collective standard of right and wrong. It deteriorates in a way similar to the situation in the book of Judges, where every man did what was right in his own eyes (Judges 21:25). When that happens, rather than focusing on the true solution to the problem, governments and their citizens wind up throwing money at things that money alone can never fix.

It's amazing how many people today believe the solution to the chaos in our country lies in more systems, or in replacing the people who perpetuate those systems. People are looking for "salvation by government." They are looking to force God's hand, way, and will into the box of elected officials. They want a kingdom they can schedule, program, and understand, thus putting their hopes in the political realm. But God warns us about what happens when we put our confidence in kings (1 Samuel 8:9-18). There is no such thing as salvation by government (Judges 8:22-23).

Yet the solutions to our nation's problems today are not going to land with Air Force One. Neither does God ride the backs of donkeys or elephants.

No party platform holds the keys to all things moral. Both major political parties have their strengths and weaknesses, depending on the issue. But both parties have also been known to simply throw money at a problem rather than seeking to radically address true change and foundational transformation. Overspending isn't a problem exclusive to one party.

The solution to our national issues will not come by pumping more money into yet another system. There are cries to change the educational system, the political system, the welfare system, the criminal justice system, the economic system, and more. We blame programs rather than people, and we fail to realize that the people themselves are creating these broken systems.

Unless you fix people, you cannot fix systems. Systems are devised not only by the people who run them but also by the people who manipulate them to their advantage. For example, between 1963 and 2010, the US government spent approximately thirteen trillion dollars attempting to fight poverty and revitalize our nation's urban communities.[7] You would think our nation could make significant progress by spending thirteen trillion dollars, right? No matter how lavish your lifestyle is, no one can spend thirteen trillion dollars and not feel it, see it, or benefit from it somehow. That's a lot of money. It's an amount beyond our comprehension.

Unless you fix people, you cannot fix systems.

Yet, our urban communities are worse off than before. During the Baltimore riots of 2015, national attention was drawn to Baltimore public schools, which no longer offered water from their drinking fountains. Due to potential contaminants in the urban school buildings' pipes, the school district had shut down the water for years. Instead, bottled water was provided to all but six of the 180 public schools. Of course, this meant rationing, inconvenience, and even a lack of dignity for thirsty students who just wanted a drink of water. The water had to be limited because bottled water was expensive ($450,000/year) and difficult to transport. It was even more difficult when the elevators were broken, as was often the case.[8]

Now, instead of urban youth reading a "Coloreds Only" sign above the water fountains (as in my parents' youth in Baltimore), kids read signs warning "Not safe to drink" posted above the fountains.

Thirteen trillion dollars later, have we come so far at all?

With trillions of dollars spent on revitalizing urban

centers, why do issues so foundational for life and dignity—such as easy access to water—even exist? The answer, as I've mentioned earlier, is not in the systems or even in the amount of money dedicated to the systems, but rather with people.

That's why it disturbs me that much of our focus during election season (or even when discussing the state of our nation) is on systems. God's problem never relates to systems. God's problem always relates to people. And, ironically, it relates to "His" people: His kingdom citizens. God is always looking for a person, or persons, through whom to usher in good.

See what God says in Jeremiah 5:1 about intervening on behalf of Jerusalem:

> Roam to and fro through the streets of Jerusalem,
> And look now and take note.
> And seek in her open squares,
> If you can find a man,
> If there is one who does justice, who seeks truth,
> Then I will pardon her.

God's intervention often comes tied to a person—a person who does justice and seeks truth. Not a system. We find a similar sentiment in Ezekiel 22:30: "I searched for a man among them who would build up the wall and stand in the gap before Me for the land, so that I would not destroy it; but I found no one."

God searched for a servant, not a system. He looked for a person, not a program. You may not like what I have to say about the solution to our nation's ills and inviting God's intervention into it, but I have been called to teach truth and not tickle ears. The solution is not out *there* where it becomes so easy to point our fingers and cast blame. The solution is in *here*—in each one of us as kingdom citizens. We have the ability to do justice, seek truth, and stand in the gap for our land. Each one of us does. The question becomes, then, are we willing? Are you?

140 Characters and 52 Days

In our fast-paced society flooded with Facebook posts, 140-character limits on Twitter, and "sermonettes," the book of Nehemiah may seem irrelevant and outdated. But no other book in the Old Testament could be more relevant than this one is to us today.

The book of Nehemiah, after all, is about a community gone bad. It is about devastation and all kinds of injustices. It is about family disintegration. You find everything in Nehemiah's story from robbery to bad interest rates to employment problems. There exist all forms of relational discord, gossip, and sabotage, and all kinds of social and psychological trauma. Every aspect of the human dilemma exists in this book.

These verses are not dusty principles and ancient insights. They hold the keys to our solution as a nation. The book of Nehemiah encourages us not to ignore the reality of the world in which we live. It also reminds us of the power of one man—or one woman. One person. Or even the collective impact of a small number of people who are seeking after God.

We can change the face of our nation.

Nehemiah was a person of vision, foresight, planning, patience, faith, impartiality, compassion, integrity, diplomacy, and persistence. This is the person God raised up to bring national change in just 52 days, despite the depths of the problems that had continued for 141 years. Why is the amount of time important to know? Because whenever you put God first and align yourself under His kingdom rule, it doesn't take long to fix anything.

We *can* change the face of our nation. We *can* avert the disastrous course of demise our country seems determined to follow. But doing so will require two things, revealed to us by a man named Nehemiah. It will require both devotion and dedication in the midst of difficulties.

The foundation of Nehemiah's narrative begins in the first chapter of the book by his name. There we discover that Nehemiah is the cupbearer to the king. Keep in mind, Nehemiah lived in the day when the nation of Israel had been overrun. In order to place this book in its proper historical setting, he lived at the same time as Daniel, Meshach, Shadrach, Abednego, Mordecai, and Esther. In fact, many believe Nehemiah received his royal appointment as cupbearer to the king because of the influence of a now aged and widowed Queen Esther.

At the time of Nehemiah, the Jewish people were still living in a pagan society under the Persian Empire. We discover how this came about by looking all the way back to King Solomon, who is described in 1 Kings 11 as a man who loved many women. These women lured his heart away from the Lord. As a result, we read:

> Now the Lord was angry with Solomon because his heart was turned away from the Lord, the God of Israel, who had appeared to him twice, and had commanded him concerning this thing, that he should not go after other gods; but he did not observe what the Lord had commanded. So the Lord said to Solomon, "Because you have done this, and you have not kept My covenant and My statutes, which I have commanded you, I will surely tear the kingdom from you, and will give it to your servant." (1 Kings 11:9-11)

Solomon's kingdom was thus divided into two: the northern kingdom, led by Jeroboam, and the southern kingdom, led by Rehoboam. In 722 BC, Assyria captured the northern kingdom. Then in 605 BC, Babylon ravaged the southern kingdom, which was the nation of Judah. The Babylonians' final invasion was carried out in 586 BC, when they ransacked Jerusalem, tore down its walls, slaughtered many people, and carried more away into captivity.

Not long after, Persia overthrew Babylon, which provided the opportunity for the people of Israel to rebuild Jerusalem. Cyrus, the premier of Persia, gave permission to the Jews that anyone who wanted to rebuild their city could do so. The first group went back under Zerubbabel in 538 BC but, due to opposition, it took them fifteen years to rebuild the temple. Another group went under Ezra's leadership in 458 BC and tried to get things right. But since the people were so morally decadent themselves, Ezra had to spend all of his time trying to get the people right with God. As a result, they made very little progress.

While the specifics may differ, the deterioration in our culture today reflects what Nehemiah faced. Nehemiah was staring straight into total community collapse, economic collapse, and social collapse, along with crime on the rampage. He belonged to a society in ruin—a society with families who could not work together or even live together.

What's more, there was no internal superstructure to

hold things in place. This was a problem politicians and economists could not solve. It was a problem social scientists and the government could not solve. Despite laws in effect, the problem of societal breakdown could not be solved.

So what did Nehemiah do?

Complain?

Blame?

Point fingers?

Divide?

Post polarizing opinions on social media?

Mock others with disrespectful memes?

Distract himself with entertainment?

No. He did none of the above.

When Nehemiah heard of the plight of his land, he took his very big problem to his even bigger God. God used Nehemiah to fix in 52 days what had lingered for 141 years. Why him? When a man or woman becomes totally available to God, things happen. Nehemiah was a kingdom man, in every sense of the word—one who also functioned as a kingdom citizen. That is why Nehemiah was used by God to change the fate and the face of his nation.

When we are introduced to Nehemiah in the first four verses of his book, his brother Hanani has come to visit. Nehemiah inquires as to the state of their "nation"—about those who managed to avoid captivity and those who sought to return. The reply came: "The remnant there in the province who survived the captivity are in great distress and reproach, and the wall of Jerusalem is broken down and its gates are burned with fire" (Nehemiah 1:3).

Hearing that his people were in ruin and their city was vulnerable to attack, Nehemiah "wept and mourned for days . . . fasting and praying before the God of heaven" (verse 4).

Reread that last line. Don't miss it. Read it again if you have to. Because the man who would go on to fix in 52 days what had been broken for 141 years gives us the strategy right from the start.

> *Nehemiah fasted and prayed and mourned, for days.*

Nehemiah fasted and prayed and mourned, *for days*. He didn't establish a committee. He didn't plan an event. He didn't hold a rally or a concert. Nehemiah didn't post a blog or even openly lament.

Now, bear in mind, we learned in the last verse of the book's opening chapter that Nehemiah was the cupbearer to the king. The cupbearer was no small position. This was a position of trust, influence, and even power. Wherever the king went, the cupbearer went. Whatever the king ate, the cupbearer ate, and he handled many of the king's administrative affairs. Nehemiah was used to this lifestyle, where one word from the king's throne changed everything instantly.

And maybe that should be our clue. Because maybe that's why Nehemiah knew how important it was to appeal to the One True King with regard to his own people. Maybe because Nehemiah saw, experienced, tasted, and lived what authority, power, and rule truly meant, he knew his greatest move to make in the face of national upheaval was to approach the throne room of his King.

So he did just that—weeping, mourning, fasting, and praying.

For days.

Consider that Nehemiah's job meant he would have been a "big shot" in his day. But he was not too "big" to pray. He was also a busy man as the cupbearer to the king. But he was not too busy to pray. Nehemiah knew that you can't fix cracks on walls, you can't fix society, and you can't even fix systems without first fixing the people within them. And you can't fix people apart from God. Thus, before Nehemiah ever came up with a "Great Society" program or before he proposed a Jerusalem "New Deal," he fasted.

He prayed.

And I don't mean just before a meal.

For days.

Prayer *is* our tool to invite heaven into history. It *is* the vehicle through which we call on the Divine to intervene in the daily. Prayer *is* the divinely authorized method to access heavenly authority for earthly intervention. It draws down the invisible into the visible. Prayer touches heaven and transforms earth.

After more than forty years of ministry, I have come to believe that prayer *is* the most underused source for accessing the spiritual authority that God has given us. It is not underused because it's unable to function as God intended, but rather because we don't understand how it works and apply it. It's also underused because we don't fully understand why prayer was designed in the first place.

The Power of Kingdom Prayer

Kingdom prayer is the established mechanism to advance God's kingdom agenda on earth. It offers access to His authority in heaven, providing the power and authority to bring it to bear on earth. In this way, God's rule is advanced in history. Kingdom prayer is all about accessing authority.

Yet we rarely think of it in that way. We rarely approach it that way.

Maybe we have not effectively used prayer because effective prayer is rooted in a devoted and dedicated relationship with the Lord. It is rooted in the abiding presence of God. It involves more than words, a location, or a desire. Powerful and life-changing, nation-changing, accessing-heaven-to-transform-societies-on-earth-changing prayer involves an ongoing, mutual relationship with God.

I say "mutual" because inherent in that is both our abiding and our alignment (obedience.) This relationship is more than merely "hanging out" with God. It is also aligning ourselves under Him.

Scripture tells us time and time again that despite Jesus' busy schedule and important demands, He frequently and continually woke up, stayed up, or went away to pray. On Christ's most difficult days, He prayed. He got up early—or stayed up late—and went away to a private place to pray.

I have experienced the power of prayer in my own life and have seen its testimony in others. When I once asked my friend Henry Blackaby, the author of the bestseller *Experiencing God*, what his secret was, he told me clearly, "I wake up at 4 a.m. and spend a couple of hours with God in prayer."

When I asked another friend and author of the life-changing book *The Prayer of Jabez* what his secret was, he said the same. Bruce Wilkinson gets up early and spends dedicated and devoted time with God in prayer. George Mueller did it. Hudson Taylor did it. Dwight L. Moody did it. Those whom God used to change nations and lives— whether in the Bible or in contemporary and historical culture—made spending time with God in prayer a priority.

On the other hand, the disciples who ran away in fear

> *On Christ's most difficult days, He prayed.*

when things got rough couldn't even pray for one hour (Matthew 26:40).

God explained the concept of abiding prayer in the book of John when Jesus spoke of a vine, branches, and fruit. Jesus is the Vine; we are the branches. Apart from Him—apart from an abiding relationship with God—we can do very little. In fact, we can't do much at all.

Apart from Me you can do nothing.

Wait, that's not what it says in John 15:5. It says we can do *nothing*.

Underline that. Understand that. Memorize that. Act on that. Live with this in mind: "I am the vine, you are the branches; he who abides in Me and I in him, he bears much fruit, for apart from Me you can do nothing." Nothing.

When we can grasp that one of the causes of our inability to strategically impact our nation for good is rooted in our own anemic engagement in personal prayer, corporate prayer, and collective prayer as the body of Christ, we will be ready to make a difference. We will be ready to, like Nehemiah, dedicate our lives to God.

Yet, there's more. There was another word related to Nehemiah—*devotion*. The term "devotion" simply means "love, loyalty or enthusiasm for another person or cause." It is hard to be devoted to another, however, when our focus is so directed at ourselves.

Did you know that a grapevine will spend most of its time and energy growing leaves when left on its own? A grapevine can produce a massive number of leaves. Yes, they will be beautiful, lush leaves draping and climbing the vine. They will even be pretty to look at.

But, because of the abundance of leaves, the grapevine will bear little or no fruit. Those lush, climbing leaves will suck the energy from the vine for their own growth while also blocking the sunlight from the grapes.

That's why a vinedresser has to cut back those leaves in order for the vine to bear fruit. Friend, I would like to suggest that we as churches have done an admirable job of growing leaves, but a less-than-admirable job of bearing fruit for the Kingdom of God.

Does it ever concern you that we have all of these churches on all of these corners with all of these programs and all of these preachers and all of these platforms and all of these people, but still have all of this mess? There's a problem somewhere. Or, even more, there is a leafy vine on the line focused on itself rather than on devotion to God and His agenda.

We must understand that the solution to the problems facing our nation today will not be found in whom we elect this voting season, although we should all vote for the candidate or candidates who best reflect the values of the Kingdom of God. Nor will the solution be found in building bigger churches or growing bigger "brands." The solution can only be found by first doing as Nehemiah did, despite his busy schedule and despite his position of notoriety in the culture. Nehemiah fell on his face before his King in dedicated and devoted humility, brokenness, and prayer.

For days.

A Kingdom Citizen's First Response

When God finds the right person, lives are fixed. Families are fixed. Churches are fixed. Even cultures and nations are fixed. While we often look at methods or try to find the best program to fix a problem, God always looks for the best person. The method, system, or solution is never as important as the person. This is because God's method *is always* a person. We are reminded in Scripture that the "eyes of the Lord" run to and fro over the earth—looking for somebody He can strengthen and use (2 Chronicles 16:9).

In short, where are our Nehemiahs today?

Who is doing what Nehemiah did? When Nehemiah heard about the collapse of his culture and the ruin of the people he loved—his community—he was so hurt and in so much pain that he fasted and prayed for days. Nehemiah didn't go to God after he tried all of his own human ingenuity or secularist thinking.

He went to God *first*.

Nehemiah's first response was prayer, devoted prayer.

Nehemiah chapter 1 records part of what he prayed. It is one of the greatest illustrations and models of prayer known to humanity. We'll read it in its entirety:

> I beseech You, O Lord God of heaven, the great and awesome God, who preserves the covenant and loving-kindness for those who love Him and keep His commandments, let Your ear now be attentive and Your eyes open to hear the prayer of Your servant which I am praying before You now, day and night, on behalf of the sons of Israel Your servants, confessing the sins of the sons of Israel which we have sinned against You; I and my father's house have sinned.
>
> We have acted very corruptly against You and have not kept the commandments, nor the statutes, nor the ordinances which You commanded Your servant Moses. Remember the word which You commanded Your servant Moses, saying, "If you are unfaithful I will scatter you among the peoples; but *if* you return to Me and keep My commandments and do them, though those of you who have been scattered were in the most remote part of the heavens, I will gather them from there and will bring them to the place where I have chosen to cause My name to dwell."

> They are Your servants and Your people whom
> You redeemed by Your great power and by Your strong
> hand. O Lord, I beseech You, may Your ear be attentive
> to the prayer of Your servant and the prayer of Your
> servants who delight to revere Your name, and make
> Your servant successful today and grant him compas-
> sion before this man. (Nehemiah 1:5-11)

Nehemiah knew that he and his culture faced a big problem. He knew that it was not solvable from a human standpoint. He understood that only when you juxtapose your greatest problem against your knowledge of the size of God can you gain a proper perspective. That is why Nehemiah began his prayer by acknowledging the greatness of God and His power over all.

You see, we are panicking in our nation today because we think our problems look so big. We panic because we don't know how we are going to get these situations fixed. We panic because we can't find a viable candidate to elect, on either side of the ticket. But I would argue that we are panicking because we fail to remember that we have a God who by His spoken word can create an entire universe. We have a God who by His own breath can transform dust into humanity. We have a God who not only made every star, but also knows them all by name.

Only when we are able to see our problems in the light

of our God will we have the confidence to move against these problems in courage, commitment, and faith.

The If/Then Clause

But Nehemiah didn't end where he began. After acknowledging the power of God, he recalled God's faithfulness, a faithfulness tied to obedience to Him. Nehemiah didn't simply call on God to fix the problem apart from his own personal responsibility and relationship to God. After all, God is not required to do anything we ask Him to do, outside of what He has already determined He will do. This is why Nehemiah tied God's faithfulness, lovingkindness, and preservation to "those who love Him and keep His commandments." God referred to this as a "covenant."

A covenant is a binding relationship that God enters into with His people. In the Bible, a covenant is a divinely created bond. It is a *spiritually binding relationship between God and His people inclusive of certain agreements, conditions, benefits, responsibilities, and effects.* God's power, provisions, and authority granted to His people operate within His covenants.

Whenever God wanted to formalize His relationship with His people, He would establish a covenant. There are a number of these agreements in Scripture, such as the Abrahamic Covenant, the Mosaic Covenant, the Davidic

Covenant, and the New Covenant. These are formal arrangements that are spiritually binding in a legal capacity between God and His people.

Nehemiah recognized the binding nature of the covenantal agreement between the Israelites and God. To those who kept God's commandments, God had legally bound Himself to preserve them. It's what is called an if/then clause. God's provisions, promises, and even His preferred will flow through the "if" of His covenant. *If* you do not operate under the terms of the covenant *then* you cannot exercise the authority granted you as a kingdom citizen in the covenant.

> *God's kingdom citizens are not functioning in concert with the covenant.*

The devil is winning much in our society and culture today because God's kingdom citizens are not functioning in concert with the covenant. Therefore, we are not benefiting from kingdom authority. It is only as we, His people, live within the context of the covenant that we will experience His covering, provision, and authority.

As we function under God and His rule, we position ourselves to be set apart for His kingdom purposes (Exodus 19:5). This is because God's covenant is specifically tied to His relationship with us in how He works both in us and through us to advance His Kingdom on earth. We are not seeing God come through for us as a culture because, by and large, we have forgotten and neglected the terms of His covenants.

Remember Nehemiah's prayer. God preserved those who "love Him and keep His commandments." God didn't preserve and protect at random.

Some of God's covenants are unconditional, yes (for example, salvation). But not all are unconditional. Many, in fact most, are conditional. These conditional covenants are predicated on our own faithfulness and obedience. As the psalmist writes, "But the lovingkindness of the Lord is from everlasting to everlasting on those who fear Him, and His righteousness to children's children, to those who keep His covenant and remember His precepts to do them" (Psalm 103:17-18).

In order to fully benefit from God's covering in our nation—His power, provisions, and authority—we must not only be *in* His covenant, but we must also align ourselves *under* His covenantal rule.

Friend, that's much more involved than attending church a couple of times a week and doing devotions for the first few minutes of the day. God must be our lifestyle, our mind-set, our very heartbeat itself. We must be willing, like the twenty-one men on the beach, to proclaim *Ya Rabbi Yasou* with regard to our finances, service, sacrifice, entertainment, purpose, prayer, commitment, words, passions, goals, and even our lives. We must be willing to break the repetitive mold of latent faith, which so often ripples atop the waters of affluence. We must be willing to pray, and then follow that prayer with action.

Finally, after witnessing the power of prayer, we see that Nehemiah's devotion led to action. Nehemiah used his leadership and administrative skills to develop a plan for restoring a broken society. He mobilized the people with a fresh vision for healing their land by prioritizing the centrality of faith in God as the foundation for their society. He also promoted the primacy of the family and the need for justice in maintaining an orderly society. Kingdom prayer must lead to kingdom action.

Like Nehemiah, we as kingdom citizens must utilize our options, skills, and positions of influence to leverage our impact in the culture. This not only includes fulfilling our responsibility to vote based on biblical values, but also supporting kingdom people who run for office. It also means getting involved with civic issues that affect our lives, families, and communities and bring a kingdom perspective to the matters at hand. Kingdom citizens must also utilize their gifts, skills and talents to expand the collective impact on their local churches' social, economic, racial, and educational benefit to their communities.

As kingdom citizens, we must promote and protect a biblical view of civil government, which is to maintain a safe, just, righteous, and compassionately responsible environment for freedom to flourish. We must be willing to truly live lives that cause those around us to watch and respond with their own commitment to Christ—with their own willingness to proclaim, "Their God is my God."

4

WHAT'S LOVE GOT TO DO WITH IT?

God has as many methods as there are stars in the sky for solving the problem of our nation's demise. After all, He is the great "un-figure-outable" God. He knows how to fix things, tweak things, and turn things that are upside down right side up again. He can turn our community unrest around on a dime, stabilize our economy, and heal racial and inequity wounds that have festered for years, or even decades and centuries. The problems come when we try to figure out how He's going to do it, or when we resist the way He plans to do it.

As a pastor, I am regularly asked by church members in difficult situations about how God might show up and transform whatever challenge they are facing. My answer is always the same. "I don't know. But what I do know is this: When God tells you to cross the Jordan, you had better start walking, and let Him work it out."

God rarely starts working it out until He sees you respond to what He has asked you to do. God responds when you walk by faith, not when you wish by faith. You can't exercise faith in a glider or an easy chair. A glider or an easy chair makes you comfortable, for sure, but it doesn't take you anywhere. Far too many believers in our nation today are satisfied with being comfortable. We like to simply push "play" and go. Check in on Sunday and coast on autopilot. But God doesn't work that way.

Drawing Close to Him

God may lead you a certain way in one situation and in a totally different way in another very similar situation. That's why we can no longer afford to be distant from Him. We must be close enough to hear from Him regularly. For example, when David fought the Philistines in the Valley of Rephaim the first time, God told him to go directly up against them and He would give them into David's hands (2 Samuel 5:17-21).

Yet in the next battle, which took place when the Philistines once again invaded the very same Valley of Rephaim, God told David, "You shall not go directly up" (verse 23). Same problem. Same location. Different solution. This time David was told to "circle around behind them and come at them in front of the balsam trees." God instructed David,

"When you hear the sound of marching in the tops of the balsam trees, then you shall act promptly, for then the LORD will have gone out before you to strike the army of the Philistines" (2 Samuel 5:23-24).

In the first battle, David was to pursue the enemy head-on. In the second battle, David was to wait until he heard the breeze blowing in the trees. I imagine that is not something David would have learned at any military academy. I am sure David never attended a class on "Breeze Blowing in the Trees Combat Strategies."

We cannot afford to be distant from God any longer.

God's ways are not our ways. Yet within the constancy of their change remains one element that never changes at all. God responds to our faith. God will frequently either increase or limit what He does in response to what we do based on what He has told us to do. Once again, that is why we cannot afford to be distant from God any longer.

There is not a one-size-fits-all prayer to fix our nation.

There is not a one-size-fits-all method to rebuild our land.

There is just the call for each of us to become a full-on, committed disciple of the King, a kingdom citizen who moves and flexes with God's will and ongoing leading. We must step in cadence with Him, staying close enough to Him to hear His every direction and call. The more of us who make this choice, the greater impact and influence we will see in our land. Will it be easy? Never. God's guidance and His plans are far different from the logic and comfort we hold dear. He demands faith because faith is His love language. He'll never call you to something you can do on your own.

> *He'll never call you to something you can do on your own.*

Focus on the fact that when God called people to do something spectacular in the Bible, the tasks He called them to were beyond them. These challenges were larger than their own skills and resources. God called Abraham to be a mighty nation. He called David to single-handedly defeat a giant more than twice his size, using an ordinary stone. He called Moses to part the Red Sea. He called Nehemiah to rebuild his nation in only fifty-two days.

You will often know God is asking you to do something if the "something" cannot be done on your own. You cannot discover how big God is unless what you need Him for is bigger than what you can produce.

People, churches, and ministries can do a number of great things in terms of our human abilities, but only God gets the glory when He pulls off what we could have never done without Him. That's why we must return to a close relationship with God. We must learn to recognize and follow His voice.

As we saw in 2 Chronicles 15, when there was no longer the true God, no longer teaching priests who taught truth, and no longer any law, there was a crisis.

But there was also a cure.

In 2 Chronicles 15:15 we read about the cure. Each person "sought Him [God] earnestly, and He let them find Him. So the Lord gave them rest on every side."

Friend, it isn't that deep. The solution to our nation's problems and unrest isn't out of reach. God hasn't hidden from us what we must do to get our country back on track. Each of us needs to seek Him earnestly, fervently, passionately, and continually.

I truly believe what we are experiencing in our nation today is intentional distress allowed by God to serve as a wake-up call to His church. Yes, the mess is happening in society, but it is also affecting each one of us. God is calling His church back to Himself to be what He created us to be and no longer to be some anomaly of religion in our culture.

Until we as individuals, and collectively as the church, return to the true God, the culture will continue to disintegrate. God won't move until we do.

God is waiting on us.

He is waiting on us since He works through the church and its members as His primary means of addressing the powers at work in the world (Ephesians 1:22-23; 3:10 and Colossians 1:15-17). This is achieved as the church develops its members into kingdom citizens who will apply a biblical worldview to every area of life.

It's Your Move

Frequently when God did something big in the Bible, He would not do it until His people moved first. Moses had to hold out the rod. Joshua had to tell the priests to put their feet in the water. Before Lazarus could emerge from his tomb, Mary had to remove the stone. God didn't move until they moved. He didn't act until He saw their faith first.

God wants to see our faith work. Faith is not a feeling. It is an action. It is something you can see take place. James tells us, "Even so faith, if it has no works, is dead, being by itself" (James 2:17). God calls us to pray, fast, and seek Him, yes. But He also wants to hear more than prayers, programs, and podcasts.

He says this clearly in Isaiah 58. The people cried to God in fasting, mourning, and great pain, but He refused to hear them. Why? Because that was not the fast He asked for (Isaiah 58:1-5). What they were doing was selfishly motivated.

They fasted, but they did not show love to the poor, the dis-enfranchised, and those who needed it most (verses 6-7).

God says a similar thing in Jeremiah 7:16: "As for you, do not pray for this people, and do not lift up cry or prayer for them, and do not intercede with Me; for I do not hear you."

God told them He would only hear them and heal their land when their actions reflected His heart of righteous-ness and justice, since both come down from His throne (Psalm 89:14). His

Faith is not a feeling. It is an action.

Word says, "For if you truly amend your ways and your deeds, if you truly practice justice between a man and his neighbor, if you do not oppress the alien, the orphan, or the widow, and do not shed innocent blood in this place, nor walk after other gods to your own ruin, then I will let you dwell in this place, in the land that I gave to your fathers forever and ever" (Jeremiah 7:5-7). Until then, they would receive His wrath.

Likewise, in Zechariah 7 we read: "'And just as He called and they would not listen, so they called and I would not lis-ten,' says the Lord of hosts; 'but I scattered them with a storm wind among all the nations whom they have not known. Thus the land is desolated behind them so that no one went back and forth, for they made the pleasant land desolate'" (verses 13-14).

Why did God not hear the cries, the calls, the prayers, the fasting of His people time and time again? Because He said that their prayers were not rooted in righteous love for Him or for others. They had what He called "hearts like flint" (Zechariah 7:12), set on their own dreams, their own purposes, pleasures, platforms, and progress. All the while ignoring the nature and truth of the living God.

Throughout the Bible, God often directly connects the impetus of His wrath being unleashed on His people to the absence of their love for one another. We learn the cure for a heart like flint when God says, "Dispense true justice and practice kindness and compassion each to his brother; and do not oppress the widow or the orphan, the stranger or the poor; and do not devise evil in your hearts against one another" (Zechariah 7:9-10). Kingdom citizens are known not only for their love for God, but also for their love for others. Also kindness. Compassion. Justice. And equity.

This is the true God.

The Role of Biblical Justice

Repeatedly throughout Scripture, God revealed Himself as a defender and deliverer. He regularly tied either a presence, or absence, of biblical justice to a presence, or absence, of His blessing and presence.

- Israel's worship was rejected because of an absence of justice in society (Amos 5:21-24).
- The Israelites were taken into captivity and held in bondage because of their rebellion against God, and they were told to practice justice and righteousness (Ezekiel 33:10-20).
- Sodom and Gomorrah were destroyed completely. And while this destruction is often attributed to the blatant practice of homosexuality, God also links His wrath toward them to their lack of concern for the poor (Ezekiel 16:49).

Time, energy, debates, blogs, and even sermons on the sin of homosexuality have focused on Sodom—one of several cities that drew down God's wrath (Jude 7). But there is an additional cause for God's judgment on Sodom. Scripture states it clearly, "Behold, this was the guilt of your sister Sodom: she and her daughters had arrogance, abundant food and careless ease, but she did not help the poor and needy" (Ezekiel 16:49). Sodom had been blessed with more than enough. And "more than enough" is not the sin. The sin is that even with "more than enough," they did not prioritize helping the poor and needy.

The prophets of the Old Testament regularly condemned the people for their social injustices as well. God's people were told to "seek the welfare" of the secular city in which they lived. They were told to pray for its well-being, and to help make it a better place to live, work, and raise children (Jeremiah 29:4-7).

We have been called as the church to carry out divine justice for the defenseless, poor, and oppressed. As participants in God's sociopolitical kingdom and as His bride, we are to do no less. After all, these are the groups Scripture focuses on because these are the groups who are the most helpless and in true need.

A strong biblical connection exists between our knowledge of and relationship with God and our concern for the poor and the oppressed (Jeremiah 22:16; Matthew 25:34-40). Micah 6:8 reveals this: "He has told you, O man, what is good; and what does the Lord require of you but to do justice, to love kindness, and to walk humbly with your God?" What does it mean to "do justice"? The word "justice" in the Bible means *to prescribe the right way*. Justice identifies the moral standard by which God measures human conduct (Isaiah 26:7-8). Biblical justice can be defined as *the equitable and impartial application of the rule of God's moral law in society, and in particular to the poor and oppressed.*

> *Justice identifies the moral standard by which God measures human conduct.*

The second-most talked about subject in Scripture, after money, is the poor. More than three hundred verses directly relate to the treatment of the poor, strategies to aid the poor, God's intentions for the poor, and what our perspective should be toward the poor. God cares about the poor. He cares deeply about those in need.

Doing justice fulfills the two greatest commandments Jesus gave us—love God and love others (Matthew 22:37-40). Christ says, "On these two commandments depend the whole Law and the Prophets." Both the content and scope of the "Law and the Prophets" were centered not only on one's relationship to God (vertical), but also on whether one was rightly related to his neighbor (horizontal).

When asked "Who is my neighbor?" (whom I am to love), Jesus responded by telling the story of the Good Samaritan, pointing out that our neighbor is the person whose need we see and whose need we are able to meet (Luke 10:26-37). Jesus concludes the story by asking us to love in like manner.

Real, Biblical Love

Love for God that does not also express itself in love for one's neighbor does not satisfy the biblical definition of love. It's simply not love. We can say we love God all day long, but when we continue to ignore the plight of the needy among us, and continue to hoard our hope as if it is ours and ours alone, we are not loving at all.

Our highest aim is to live as a model—a *horizontal Jesus*—to others, thus reflecting His love.

What is biblical love? Love is *compassionately and righteously pursuing the well-being of another.* Therefore, since loving one's neighbor includes seeking his best interest by rescuing him from injustice or oppression, and we are able to do just that, then we validate our love for God through this liberating love for others.

Jesus' earthly ministry to people consistently modeled this for us:

- Jesus lived among the oppressed (Luke 13:22-34)
- Jesus fed those who needed food (Luke 9:10-17)
- Jesus restored the needy (Luke 5:12-16)
- Jesus healed the sick and hurting (Luke 7:18-23)

All of Jesus' good works were clearly connected to the spiritual purposes of God (Matthew 4:23-24).

John, the apostle, also stressed the importance of love in authenticating spirituality and religion. "If someone says, 'I love God,' and hates his brother, he is a liar; for the one who does not love his brother whom he has seen, cannot love God whom he has not seen" (1 John 4:20). John reminded us that this love is to be expressed through actions and not just words as it is carried out in "deed and truth" (1 John 3:18).

James emphasized this further. "Did not God choose the poor of this world to be rich in faith and heirs of the kingdom which He promised to those who love Him?" (James 2:5). He also defines true religion by how one treats the widow and the orphan (James 1:27).

This same emphasis continued in the early church. This church turned the world upside down due to its love (Acts 17:6). It brought joy to an entire city (Acts 8:8). In short, it was known for its good works (Acts 4:32-35; 5:11-16). And these good works were not only for church members; they were for all people in need (Galatians 6:10).

Love is foundational to fulfilling the purpose of the church.

Love—in the form of social action—isn't simply to be relegated to a special event or a holiday food drive. Love is foundational to fulfilling the purpose of the church as intimated by the heart of God. It is a result of God's people becoming one through being what God has called us to be, and participating in what He has called us to do—reflect His light through love. And it is sorely missing in our country today. We, like Sodom, have ignored the plight of the poor while building and buying all we want for ourselves, and then some (Haggai 1:4).

A community with a church in its midst should be better off because of the church's presence. More so, a country with hundreds of thousands of churches in its midst should be better off because of them. Its citizens should feel, sense, see, and experience the impact of our intentional and ongoing love for others, particularly for those in need.

The bottom line is this: we can have all the convocations we want. We can pray all we want. We can fast all we want. We can do all the stuff we want and stand before the courthouses of our nation in droves protesting or praying. It doesn't really matter on its own.

Because if we do not have love, compassion, equity, and kindness with and for one another, particularly for those who need it most—the oppressed, disenfranchised, poor, and vulnerable—God Himself says He will not listen. He will be our problem because we will have become nothing more than annoying gongs and clanging cymbals (1 Corinthians 13:1).

What then must we do to reverse our nation's downward spiral? What can you do as a kingdom citizen to rebuild our broken nation?

We must do as Nehemiah did. You must do as Nehemiah did. We must do as the twenty-one men did on the beach in Libya. We must do as the church in Acts did. We must do as David did. As Esther did.

We must do as Jesus did. As Jesus does.

We must fully commit our lives, time, hearts, money, focus, intentions, brands, resources, platforms, hope, goals, prayers, choices, and churches to the King and His kingdom agenda. We, His kingdom citizens, must put God first. And subsequently, put all others second. Yes, even before ourselves.

What's love got to do with it?

What's love got to do with rebuilding our nation?

Everything.

Love God *first*. Love others *second*. Then watch what God will do.

5

A Closing Thought

April 4, 1968, and the days that followed . . .

As a seventeen-year-old boy, I sat staring out our house window upon row after row of National Guardsmen lining our street. Baltimore had become a swarm of soldiers—a bastion of privileged power. They stood strong as columns—uniformed officers covering the paths of this city once known for its lure, literature, jazz, and baseball. They remained on guard, ready and willing to defend against people who looked like me—a black, teenaged male in the midst of a country divided by color.

The assassination of Martin Luther King Jr. had led to explosive riots in our city. As a result, we (Black Americans) were immediately placed under curfew, evoking fear in most of us. This fear came laced with confusion regarding the authenticity and integrity of those who touted our country as "one nation under God."

The siege lasted more than a week. It felt like a year. I

barely left my parents' row house for fear of being mistaken as a protestor intent on disruption. My mother, father, brothers, sister, and I holed up together, huddling as hostages in our own home, hoping and praying for this nightmare to somehow end.

My mother, father, brothers, sister, and I holed up together.

After many long days, peace was restored, and the National Guardsmen funneled out. They had made their point. There would be no ongoing rioting to protest the loss of one of our nation's most peaceful promoters of equity. Not on their watch. After all, this was Baltimore—once dubiously dubbed "Charm City" by advertisers and marketers seeking to put a new spin on a very old reality using a few choice words.

Yet as history told us, and as our future would also reveal, it required more than a few words to change what took years, even decades, to produce.

The year 1968 wasn't the first time Baltimore faced riots, disunity, or destruction. Neither had its problems always been based on race. On July 20, 1877, the governor of Maryland called up the National Guard to defend against striking white citizens who were protesting lowered wages for the Baltimore & Ohio Railroad workers. This riot rained bullets as National Guardsmen fired into the crowds, killing ten and wounding dozens.

Step back further in time to the War of 1812, a war commemorated on license plates all across Maryland. This war saw the British bombing Baltimore, bombarding it and her citizens with a hailstorm of destruction, fire, and the sheer madness of battle.

This very confrontation gave us one of our nation's greatest songs. We all sing it, often without thinking. It opens our sporting events and sometimes our schools. The lyrics, penned by Francis Scott Key, speak of freedom, peace, bravery, and unity—reminding us that we are all entwined within the success (or demise) of our nation together. Or as Martin Luther King Jr. penned it, together we comprise an "inescapable network of mutuality . . . [our] single garment of destiny." As he emphasized elsewhere, "Whatever affects one directly, affects all indirectly. . . . This is the interrelated structure of reality."

The injustices and the chaos of 1812, 1877, 1968, and even those that lit the city afire again in 2015 in Baltimore, affect us all. And they arise from us all. They arise from the collective conscience of a nation too often out of step with God's overarching and comprehensive rule. *Collective conscience* does not only refer to the politicians who govern us or the laws that bind us. It refers to each one of us as citizens of our nation. We all live, exist, and pursue our dreams in this *interrelated structure of reality*. Thus, when we face issues on every corner and ruin throughout our land, we have to look within at what we can do to effect and influence change for good rather than pointing fingers at others and complaining about how bad things are now.

After all, it seems we have become a nation of complainers and criticizers, despite Christ's command of compassion. I'll never forget sitting at a lunch with a group of prominent Christian leaders the day the Baltimore riots broke out in 2015. Most of those at the table were white. The conversation drifted quickly away from the reasons the riots erupted in the first place to things like the supposed injustice of having to close down the Baltimore Orioles stadium to fans. "Now, look what's happened," one person said. "Fans can't even go to the game. This is ridiculous! This has really gotten out of hand." That person was serious.

Then another lunch guest lamented that he had planned a trip to Baltimore in the near future and would be saddened if Orioles Park was not open by then. I quickly realized how unaware many people are of true injustice and how intrinsically related we are to each other.

Real problems brought on the riots. Of course no one condones rioting, but to ignore the reality of hopelessness and systemic injustices that produced it is to live in an intentionally naive state. Individuals and families faced real problems on a scale much larger than the inability to attend a baseball game.

What struck me as even more ironic about the baseball-game comments was remembering the song that is sung at each game. A song that was birthed in a riot and battle for justice. A song birthed in Baltimore and containing these words, which are supposed to apply to us all:

And this be our motto: "In God is our trust."

In God is our trust.

One nation under God.

How quickly we throw out these phrases. Or seek to use them to our advantage when we feel our rights as people of faith are being infringed upon. But do we, as believers, behave in ways that reflect these phrases? How can we be one nation under God if we cannot even be one church under God? How can we expect compassion in our culture if we do not even have it ourselves?

How can we be one nation under God if we cannot even be one church under God?

I close with this story not to judge or cast blame, but to enlighten. It's to cast a mental framework for how believers are called to something better in our behavior and attitudes. As believers, our lack of understanding and empathy for people and their problems in our nation has much to do with the pulpit's failure to make Jesus' example the centerpiece for all we are. Rather than grab basins and towels, we've built buildings and brands. Rather than promote humility and compassion, we've made platforms and honored pride.

But this book is not about race. It is about the devolving state of our nation and what we, as believers, can and should do to stop it.

However, this well-known melting pot of inequity, judgment, and apathy that too often describes the American church sheds light on why we are losing the fight. If we cannot even be one church under God, how can we call our country to be one nation under God?

If there is one thing election season teaches us, it is that many, if not most, of us come to the topics at hand with very strong opinions about them and about each other. We label everything from laws to lawmakers to leaders to life itself. Thus, we divide far faster than we unite (John 17:21). We cast stones further than any nets (Mark 1:17).

As a result, we—who call ourselves the body of Jesus Christ—are having, at best, an anemic impact on our culture and our nation for good. At worst, we are actively contributing to its demise.

And, worse yet, we have lost claim to the one label by which God created us to ascribe: Love.

I have chosen to speak of Martin Luther King Jr. because of a recent visit I made to his memorial and what I was reminded of that day. Earlier this year I was honored to deliver the message and the prayer at the National Day of Prayer invocation in Washington, DC. It was a meaningful event, and I'm grateful to have participated. While there, I took time to visit the monument to Martin Luther King Jr. With my busy work and travel schedule, this was my first opportunity to go.

I was deeply affected by seeing this monument to Dr. King, reminded of what he stood for and achieved, not only for me and for my family, but for all Black Americans. I'll never forget the emotions that welled up as I walked closer and saw both the mountain and the statue of this great man. Experiencing it for the first time reminded me of the core of his message—a message we would do well to adopt today. Because his was a message of *love*.

> *I was deeply affected by seeing this monument to Dr. King.*

It was as if I were hearing him speak again for the first time—as I did on August 28, 1963. I don't know if you remember where you were on that day, but I do. I sat spellbound in front of the television, tears welling up in my eyes as I heard his vision for freedom. To see how he so eloquently captured and encapsulated the comprehensive context of our nation amazed me.

He called out for freedom.

He cried out for futures.

He dared to dream.

But what struck me the most, as I stood before this statue in our nation's capital earlier this year, was the beautiful thing about Dr. King. All he did and strove for was always covered and couched in love. He refused to bow to voices and principles of hate, though humanly speaking there was a lot to react to emotionally. Rather, he saw the biblical principle of *love* as the all-encompassing illustration and story to tell.

His call to a people struggling for freedom then is no less needed today as a call and reminder for many of us struggling to defend religious freedom and liberty:

> *Let no man pull you so low as to hate him.*
> After all, *Darkness cannot drive out darkness.*
> *Only light can do that. Hate cannot drive out hate.*
> *Only love can do that.*

Rather than focusing on what is wrong with our nation and bemoaning the depths to which we as a nation have fallen, we would do well to live in light of Martin Luther King's call. *We would do well to love.* We would do well to focus on what is right with God and how He can reverse what is wrong in our land. We would do well to *be* the light that drives out the darkness.

Only a few people like Martin Luther King Jr., in the face of hate, injustice, disagreement, and persecution, responded with love in their day. It seems like there are even fewer today.

Spend ten minutes perusing social media sites (even, if not especially, those of Christians) and you will quickly see some of the most debasing, critical, and insulting forms of language and images related to our nation and/or politics. Especially regarding the 2016 presidential election.

Visit any church on any Sunday and you will (99 times out of 100) discover that 11 a.m. on Sunday morning is still the most segregated hour in America. I still cannot fully understand how we can so easily cheer a secular sports team comprised of all races and yet continue to go to our separate corners to worship.

Something is amiss in our faith and its translation to our feet.

Something is amiss in the core of our Christianity, a core that ought to be pregnant with compassion, light, and love.

Will you be the one to drive out darkness with your light?

Something is amiss in our souls.

Martin Luther King Jr.'s dream was not for himself. It was for others. It was for generations to come. Dare we dream beyond our own four walls and cushioned pews? Dare we dream beyond our own brands and buildings? Dare we do the diligent and devoted work of kingdom citizens so those who come after us will be able to dream at all?

As I stood in the shadow of the statue of a man God

used to call a nation to change for good, I remembered how throughout the Bible, God always looks for a person He can use to change a nation or the land. In the midst of upheaval, confusion, and chaos, God has a pattern of finding a person or persons, and using them to alter the landscape of a country.

He did it with Moses.

He did it with Joshua.

He did it with David. Esther. Jeremiah. Daniel. Elijah. Deborah.

And Nehemiah.

He can also do it with you. Will you be the one? Will you be the one to drive out darkness with your light? Will you be the one to combat judgment with your love? Will you be the one to seek God with your whole heart and being?

Will you be the one to help rebuild our broken land?

Anthony T. Evans
Dallas, Texas

THREE-PART PLAN FOR NATIONAL CULTURAL TRANSFORMATION

In all times, but especially in turbulent and trying times, we need a national strategy that can be implemented on the local level and led by churches.

Phase one of my proposed strategy involves calling a solemn assembly. A solemn assembly is a sacred gathering called by God's people with the intent of inviting the return of His manifest presence back into the midst of His people. Through them, it will overflow into the broader society.

The purpose of a solemn assembly is restoring God's people through the repentance of their sins and the passionate pursuit of the return of His presence among them. Priests, prophets, and kings in the Bible often called these assemblies during times of national crisis.

Although the term "solemn assembly" may seem foreign to many Christians, there are several examples in the Old Testament: Samuel, Jehoshaphat, Josiah, Joel, and others called solemn assemblies. In the New Testament, the first Christians were gathering in a solemn assembly when they received the Holy Spirit at Pentecost.

In fact, American history shows that prior to every spiritual awakening, beginning with the great revival led by Jonathan Edwards in colonial times, the spiritual leadership of the day placed a strong emphasis on fasting and gathering for solemn assemblies.

From the Garden in Genesis to the heavens in Revelation, God ushers a call time and again for reconciliation before issuing judgment. He is swift to spare if each of us will but ask Him for a new heart and new spirit as His prescribed pathway to seeing hope restored and lives transformed.

Nothing is ever too far gone or so out of reach that God cannot revive it. Yet to turn our nation to God, we—His people—will need to make a collective effort to return to Him first.

Phase two in this overarching strategy is to move from an emphasis in our churches on church membership to church discipleship. This is where the primary objective shifts to an intentional focus on leading and shepherding believers to learn how to progressively bring all of life under the lordship of Jesus Christ.

One of the primary reasons the collective church in America has been less effective in positively influencing the culture for good on a large and ever-increasing scale is our failure to produce disciples. We have somehow created Jesus fans rather than fully committed Jesus followers. A disciple is a Christian who is progressively bringing every area of life under the lordship of Jesus Christ. Discipleship involves that process of the local church to move Christians from spiritual infancy to spiritual maturity so that they are able to reproduce the process with someone else.

In order to achieve this goal, the church must provide the primary collective context for its members to share in the four biblical experiences. These four biblical experiences include: (1) worship, which is the recognition of God for who He is, what He has done, and what He promises to do; (2) fellowship, which includes the mutual sharing of the life and love of Christ among the members; (3) education, which is the teaching and training of a biblical worldview and its application to every area of life; and (4) outreach, which involves the witnesses of the gospel and biblical and spiritual truths to the unsaved in both word and deed.

The various ministries, teaching, and objectives of the church must focus on helping believers to function as children of the King where His rule reigns paramount. When this is done, the power, presence, and authority of Christ are being transferred and modeled in every aspect of their lives. Without discipleship, which is at the heart of the Great Commission, there is no authorized vehicle through which Christ can influence the culture.

In the third and final phase of the strategy churches unite across racial, cultural, and class lines to collectively influence their local communities through a common impact initiative. This local influence will collectively overflow to impact the nation. Whether these initiatives include the adoption of public schools or adoption of city blocks—the key is churches working together on common goals that benefit their communities. For example, at our church in Dallas, where every member is expected to serve, we challenge church members to respond to community needs personally, as a regular lifestyle. We encourage them to meet a specific need, offer to pray for the person whose need they met, then look for an opportunity to share the gospel.

In addition, our single church has officially adopted over 50 public schools, something we have done for nearly three decades. This adoption consists of initiatives where our members provide mentoring and family support services to the at-risk students and their parents in those schools. These services also include tutoring, job training and placement, GED counseling, crisis intervention, housing for the homeless, mentoring through athletics, pregnancy intervention, school assemblies, parenting education, back-to-school rallies at our church where we present the gospel, economic development, a credit union, and a thrift store. Hundreds of church members participate in these outreach initiatives weekly.

We also seek to have church representatives in the political, social, educational, and economic places in our community and to disciple them as they serve in these roles. These representatives keep the church abreast of issues in our community and act as liaisons from the church to speak into those issues from a kingdom perspective. In addition to discipling individuals to make an impact, we ask our small groups and ministry groups to adopt projects designed to meet pressing needs in the lives of those around them and in neighboring areas.

Through our national ministry, The Urban Alternative, we assist churches in developing their members into disciples who will function as kingdom citizens. We do this through online training, resources, on-site seminars and by producing college and seminary coursework on community-impact strategies. We also bring churches together across social, racial, and cultural lines to mobilize their kingdom citizens to adopt schools in their communities and provide similar services for the well-being of their communities. Racial reconciliation is best achieved through service, not through seminars.

All of these efforts are to be viewed as part of being a public representative of the Kingdom of God, whose job is not only to impact the church but also to transform the community to insure that both righteousness and justice—particularly on behalf of the poor, oppressed, and downtrodden—are being promoted and maintained in society.

God's people are called to actively seek the well-being of the community in which they exist. Only by our active involvement as kingdom citizens can we expect to see God's hand bring order to a culture in chaos (Jeremiah 29:7).

PRAYERS FOR AMERICA

Let us continue to pray for our country and its future. These prayers from respected Christian leaders powerfully express the feelings, trust, petitions, and praise we share in challenging times. Use them to help you pray or to inspire your own prayers for America.

⸺

Lord God,

You tell us to pray for all those in authority, and so we respectfully ask for Your convicting, converting, and disciplining hand to be upon those in power. Many of our leaders are unaware that You can "turn the hearts of kings," so raise Yourself preeminent in their thoughts and intents—and if any leader persists in dishonoring and disregarding Your precepts, either restrain them or remove them. Open paths for godly leaders, and bring down in shame those who resist Your ways. We ask You to make us strong in Christ so that if oppression increases, we may choose our Lord and Master over every comfort. May Your mighty work be accomplished in our nation, despite evil ascending. You have done this before in other lands, and we pray You will do it again in our great country, for the glory of Christ.

> Joni Eareckson Tada
> Joni and Friends International Disability Center

Father God,

Thank You that we live in a country that was birthed out of a desire for freedom from tyranny and religious oppression. For our founding fathers and those who have walked before us, we give You thanks. Today, we again face tyranny and religious oppression. We confess that as a nation, we have gone our own way and ignored Your principles of morality and justice. We have put our judgments above Your commands. May Your Spirit touch our hearts and bring us to repentance, knowing that Your mercy is always extended when we turn to You.

I pray for our fractured families: for those who have gone through the trauma of divorce; for children who are growing up without a father; for single moms who face the challenge of parenting alone. I pray that You will bring comfort and direction to all who feel unloved. Stir the hearts of Your people that we may be agents of love and hope; that we will seek Your plans for our role in Your kingdom and in our culture. Give us courage to speak the truth in love. May our lifestyle demonstrate that we are followers of Christ.

We acknowledge that You instituted human government for the good of mankind. Now, I pray that You will raise up leaders on every level who will see themselves as public servants committed to the well-being of all citizens. May we again see ourselves as "one nation under God with liberty and justice for all."

> Gary D. Chapman, Ph.D.
> Author, speaker, pastor

Lord of the Universe. Lord of this planet. Lord of the nations. Lord of our hearts.

We look to You . . .

When there is anarchy on our streets and arrogance in our leadership,

When there is apostasy in the church and apathy in the people,

When businesses are bankrupted, trust is betrayed, and jobs are lost,

When threats, violence, and terrorists produce a death rattle in the very heart of our nation.

You are the Rock on which we stand.

We make our prayer to You using the words of the prophet Daniel: O Lord, You are the great and awesome God, who keeps His covenant of love with those who love Him and keep His commandments. You are merciful and forgiving. You are righteous, but this day we are covered with shame because we have sinned against You and done wrong. We have turned away from Your commands and principles. We have turned away from You.

As a result, You have sought our attention by bringing against us great disasters. Under the whole heaven when has there ever been done to our nation like what has been done in the attack on 9/11? Or the breaking of the levees in New Orleans? Or the fires of Southern California? Or the floods of West Virginia? Or the carnage in San Bernardino and Orlando? At the same time we are burdened by a depressed economy that has left millions jobless, and divided by a deep bitterness that has left many hopeless. All these disasters have come on us, yet we have not sought the favor of the Lord our God by turning from our sins and giving attention to Your truth.

Yet You have promised in 2 Chronicles 7 when disasters strike, that if we—a people identified with You—would humble ourselves, pray, seek Your face, and turn from our wicked ways, then You would hear our prayer, forgive our sin and heal our land.

So we choose to stop pointing our finger at the sins of others, and examine our own hearts and lives. We choose to acknowledge our own sin—our neglect and defiance and ignorance and even rejection of You. This day we choose to repent.

In response to our heartfelt repentance, God of Abraham, Isaac and Jacob, Father of Jesus Christ, in keeping with all Your righteous acts and according to Your promise, turn away Your anger and Your wrath from the United States of America. Hear the prayers and petitions offered to You, as we give You our full attention. Give ear, our God, and hear; open Your eyes and see. We do not make requests of You because we are righteous, but because of Your great mercy.

For the glory of Your Name hear our prayer, forgive our sin, and heal our land.

We ask this in the name of Your Son Jesus Christ who offers us salvation from Your judgment, forgiveness for our sin, and reconciliation with You through His own blood shed on the Cross. Amen

Anne Graham Lotz
Honorary Chairman,
National Day of Prayer Task Force, 2014

Father in Heaven,

Help us remember that, as Your peculiar people, we Christians have always been strangers and sojourners on the earth. Remind us that it is not our job to direct the destinies of nations, but simply to shine for You, reflect Your image, and bloom for Christ wherever You choose to plant us. In that spirit, inspire us to seek our country's peace and wellbeing, even as Jeremiah instructed the Jewish exiles to work for the peace of the city to which they had been carried captive. Teach us to pray to You consistently on its behalf, knowing that in its welfare we will find peace for ourselves. Never let us forget that, come what may, our calling is always to obey God rather than man.

>Jim Daly
>President and CEO, Focus on the Family

Almighty Father,

We come before You aware of the fact that government is not an accident nor is it our invention, but rather it is Your gift to us in the very structures of creation as You have given us—that which will lead to righteousness and justice and human flourishing. We understand that You have created government and given it to us, Your human creatures, in order to restrain evil and uphold that which is good.

Father, You have placed us in a time and in a season where we are allowed the privilege of participating in our government. Lord, we pray that we would steward the responsibilities of our democracy well. We pray we would discharge our responsibilities as citizens in a way that honors You and magnifies Your sovereignty and kingship over all.

Father, You have set forth in Scripture a model of the kind of leaders we should aspire to have—leaders who uphold righteousness and justice and who exercise mercy and compassion for destitute and oppressed.

Father we pray that You will give us leaders, congressman, senators, justices, and presidents, who will uphold righteousness and do justice and whose personal character will befit their office. We pray for leaders whose convictions and understanding will lead to flourishing in our nation.

Father, we pray for the sanctity of human life to be upheld. We pray for leaders who value the dignity of every human life. We pray for the least of these among us to be protected. We pray for a government and for leaders who will unite us and who will truly pursue justice for all.

Finally, Lord, we pray for a government that fulfills its commission with integrity and righteousness. We acknowledge that we do not always deserve such a government. But we pray in confidence knowing that it is not we who rule, but You. We commit ourselves and our nation to You as Your thankful people.

In Christ's name we pray. Amen.

Dr. R. Albert Mohler, Jr.

President, Southern Baptist Theological Seminary

Dear Heavenly Father,

We come to You today as a humble people desperate for Your supernatural intervention on behalf of our beloved nation. First, we thank You for all the blessings You have bestowed on our land, blessings that have allowed us to bring so much good and benefit to not only our own citizens but also to the rest of the world. The very ideals upon which this country was founded were based on biblical truths, no matter how some try to rewrite history to deny that very fact today.

This is why our hearts are so broken over how You continue to be marginalized and dismissed by both our people and our institutions. We are also saddened by the fact that Your people have contributed greatly to the spiritual apathy that now engulfs us. Our satisfaction in remaining religious without being fully committed to living out the truths of Your Word has caused us to become co-conspirators with the forces of evil that are destroying us as a society.

It is for this reason that we personally and collectively repent of our carnality and recommit ourselves to becoming visible and verbal disciples of Jesus Christ. Enable us, by Your Spirit, to no longer be secret agent Christians but rather to publicly declare and live out Your truth in a spirit of love so that You feel welcome in our country once again.

Thank You for Your promise to hear our prayers when we call to You with hearts of repentance and obedience, which is how we are appealing to You today, Father. On behalf of Your church, we affirm afresh the priority You are to us that You would fill every dimension of our lives as we seek to bring You glory through the advancement of Your kingdom in our personal lives, our family lives, and in the lives of our churches and our government leaders. We confidently invite heaven's intervention into all the affairs of our nation and we praise You in advance for Your answer.

In Jesus' name we pray. Amen.

Dr. Tony Evans

Honorary Chairman,

National Day of Prayer Task Force, 2016

QUESTIONS TO CONSIDER

These questions have two purposes. First, they can help you dig more deeply into this book and personally apply the concepts and principles to your individual life and the world around you. Second, they can serve as discussion-starters among friends and family, or even for a Bible study group. May they be useful tools as you seek God's leading and fulfill your role as a kingdom citizen.

Chapter 1: See That Mess? Blame Me

1. The definition of a kingdom citizen is *a visible, verbal follower of Jesus Christ who consistently applies the principles of heaven to the concerns of culture.* In your opinion, which "concerns of culture" most need to be addressed in your life, your community, and our nation?
2. When was the last time your relationship with Christ was visible and/or verbal?
3. What is the difference between hearing God's Word and being transformed by it?

4. What is your responsibility when it comes to functioning as a kingdom citizen? What does that look like in your own world?

5. What does it mean to "fiercely return to God"? What changes can you make to help you move closer to Him?

6. How might you better align your time, thoughts, talents, and treasures under God?

Chapter 2: Selfies or Service

1. Is there anything about the way you live that would cause a non-believer to say, "Your God is my God"?

2. What difference does it make in your understanding of the Bible when you consider its unifying central theme?

3. Is God's rule ever sidelined in your life? Where and when?

4. Where does your church body make the most impact? Does it ever lack impact in certain areas? Why?

5. Are you growing as a disciple of Jesus Christ? Why or why not?

6. If the church is God's "levee," how are you helping to strengthen it?

Chapter 3: A Servant, Not a System

1. "Unless you fix people, you cannot fix systems."
   What is an example of this truth in your world?
2. Have you ever depended on cultural systems to "fix"
   issues in your life? In what way?
3. If you are willing to "do justice, seek truth, and stand
   in the gap for our land," how can you begin—or
   move further toward that goal?
4. What is at the foundation of effective prayer?
5. When have you personally experienced the power
   of prayer?
6. What changes might you make in your own prayer
   life to grow in devotion and bear fruit?
7. As a kingdom citizen, how can you best use your
   options, skills, and influence to affect our culture?

Chapter 4: What's Love Got to Do with It?

1. Is there a big task God is calling you to do? Have you
   prayed about it? Do you trust He will equip you to
   answer His call?
2. "Faith is not a feeling. It is an action." What does this
   statement mean to you?
3. What is the cure for a "heart like flint"?

4. What aspects of your life visibly express love for the defenseless, poor, and oppressed?

5. What changes do you need to make to better "love your neighbor"?

6. How will loving God and loving your neighbor affect your family, your community, and your country?

Chapter 5: A Closing Thought

1. Think of a time you chose complaint over compassion. What happened? Did it help solve a problem or make you feel better?

2. When did you choose to show compassion in a difficult situation? What was the outcome?

3. When people judge you or act hatefully toward you, how do you typically respond? What feelings come into the situation? What actions do you take, or resist taking?

4. "Light can drive out darkness." How can your decisions and actions bring light to darkness today? Next week? In the year ahead?

THE URBAN ALTERNATIVE

The Urban Alternative (TUA), founded by Dr. Tony Evans, *equips*, *empowers*, and *unites* Christians to impact *individuals*, *families*, *churches*, and *communities* through a thoroughly kingdom agenda worldview. In teaching truth, we seek to transform lives.

The core cause of the problems we face in our personal lives, homes, churches, and societies is spiritual; therefore, the only way to address our problems is through a spiritual solution. We've tried a political, social, economic, and even a religious agenda.

It's time for a *kingdom agenda*. *The Kingdom agenda can be defined as the visible manifestation of the comprehensive rule of God over every area of life.*

The unifying central theme throughout the Bible is the glory of God and the advancement of His Kingdom. The Word of God from Genesis to Revelation—from beginning to end—is focused on one thing: God's glory through advancing God's Kingdom.

Without that theme, the Bible becomes a series of disconnected stories that are great for inspiration but appear unrelated in purpose and direction. The Bible exists to share God's movement in history toward the establishment and expansion of His Kingdom. Understanding that theme increases the relevancy of this several-thousand-year-old manuscript to your day-to-day living, because the kingdom was not only then, but it is also now.

The absence of the Kingdom's influence in our personal and family lives, churches, and communities has led to a deterioration of immense proportions in our world:

- People live segmented, compartmentalized lives because they lack God's kingdom worldview.
- Families disintegrate because they exist for their own satisfaction rather than for the Kingdom.
- Churches are limited in the scope of their impact because they fail to comprehend that the church's goal is not the church itself, but the Kingdom.
- Communities have nowhere to turn to find real solutions for real people who have real problems, because the church has become divided, ingrown, and unable to transform the cultural landscape in any relevant way.

The kingdom agenda offers us a way to see and live life with a solid hope by optimizing the solutions of heaven. When God, and His rule, are no longer the final and authoritative standard under which everything else exists, then order and hope leave along with Him. However, the reverse of that is true as well: As long as you have God, you have hope. If God is still in the picture, and as long as His agenda is still on the table, it's not over.

Even if relationships collapse, God will sustain you. Even if finances dwindle, God will keep you. Even if dreams die, God will revive you. As long as God, and His rule, are still the overarching rule in your life, family, church, and community, there is always hope.

Our world needs the King's agenda. Our churches need the King's agenda. Our families need the King's agenda.

In many major cities, drivers can take a loop or bypass when they want to get to the other side of the city, but don't necessarily want to head straight through downtown. This loop will take drivers close enough to the heart of the city that they can see its towering buildings and skyline, but not close enough to actually experience it.

This is precisely what we, as a culture, have done with God. We have put Him on the "loop" of our personal, family, church, and community lives. He's close enough to be at hand should we need Him in an emergency, but far enough away that He can't be the center of who we are.

We want God on the "loop," not the King of the Bible who comes "downtown" into the very heart of our ways. Leaving God on the loop brings about dire consequences, as we have seen in our own lives and with others. But when we make God, and His rule, the centerpiece of all we think, do, or say, then we will experience Him in the way He longs to be experienced by us.

He wants us to be kingdom people with kingdom minds set on fulfilling His kingdom's purposes. He wants us to pray, as Jesus did, "Not my will, but Thy will be done." Because His is the Kingdom, the power, and the glory.

There is only one God, and we are not Him. As King and Creator, God is in charge. Only when we align ourselves underneath His comprehensive hand will we access His full power and authority in all spheres of life—personal, familial, church, and community.

As we learn how to govern ourselves under God, we then transform the institutions of family, church, and society through a biblically based kingdom worldview.

Under Him, we touch heaven and change earth.

To achieve our goal we use a variety of strategies, approaches, and resources for reaching and equipping as many people as possible.

Broadcast Media

Millions of individuals experience *The Alternative with Tony Evans* through the daily radio broadcast, playing on nearly one thousand radio outlets and in more than one hundred countries. The broadcast can also be seen on several television networks and is viewable online at TonyEvans.org. You can also listen to or view the daily broadcast by downloading the Tony Evans app for free in the App store. More than four million message downloads occur each year.

Leadership Training

The *Tony Evans Training Center* (TETC) facilitates educational programming that embodies the ministry philosophy of Dr. Tony Evans as expressed through the kingdom agenda. The training courses focus on leadership development and discipleship in the following five tracks:

1. Bible and Theology
2. Personal Growth
3. Family and Relationships
4. Church Health and Leadership Development
5. Society and Community Impact Strategies

The TETC program includes courses for both local and online students. Furthermore, TETC programming includes course work for non-student attendees. Pastors, Christian leaders, and Christian laity, both local and at a distance, can seek out the Kingdom Agenda Certificate for personal, spiritual, and professional development. Some courses are valued for CEU credit as well as viable in transferring for college credit with our partner school(s).

Kingdom Agenda Pastors (KAP) provides a viable network for like-minded pastors who embrace the kingdom agenda philosophy. Pastors have the opportunity to go deeper with Dr. Tony Evans as they gain greater biblical knowledge, understand practical applications, and receive resources to impact individuals, families, churches, and communities. KAP welcomes senior and associate pastors of all churches. KAP also offers an annual summit held each year in Dallas with intensive seminars, workshops, and resources.

Pastors' Wives Ministry, founded by Dr. Lois Evans, provides counsel, encouragement, and spiritual resources for pastors' wives as they serve with their husbands in the ministry. A primary focus of the ministry is the KAP summit, which offers senior pastors' wives a safe place to reflect, renew, and relax along with training in personal development, spiritual growth, and care for their emotional and physical well-being.

Community Impact

National Church Adopt-A-School Initiative (NCAASI) prepares churches across the country to influence communities by using public schools as the primary vehicle for effecting positive social change in urban youth and families. Leaders of churches, school districts, faith-based orga-nizations, and other nonprofit organizations are equipped with the knowledge and tools to forge partnerships and build strong, social service delivery systems. This training is based on the comprehensive church-based community impact strategy conducted by Oak Cliff Bible Fellowship. It addresses such areas as economic development, education, housing, health revitalization, family renewal, and racial reconciliation. We assist churches in tailoring the model to meet specific needs of their communities while simulta-neously addressing the spiritual and moral frame of refer-ence. Training events are held annually in the Dallas area at Oak Cliff Bible Fellowship.

Athlete's Impact (AI) exists as an outreach both into and through the sports arena. Coaches are the most influential factor in young people's lives, even ahead of their parents. With the growing rise of fatherlessness in our culture, more young people are looking to their coaches for guidance, character development, practical needs, and hope. Ath-letes are next on the influencer scale after coaches. Athletes (whether professional or amateur) influence younger ath-letes and kids within their spheres of impact. Knowing this, we have made it our aim to equip and train coaches and athletes on how to live out and utilize their God-given roles for the benefit of the kingdom. We aim to do this through our iCoach App, weCoach (Football) Conference, as well as resources such as *The Playbook: A Life Strategy Guide for Athletes*.

Resource Development

We are fostering lifelong learning partnerships with the people we serve by providing a variety of published materials. Dr. Evans has published more than one hundred unique titles based on more than forty years of preaching in booklet, book, and Bible study formats. The goal is to strengthen individuals in their walk with God and service to others.

For more information and a complimentary copy
of Dr. Evans' devotional newsletter,
call (800) 800-3222,
write TUA at PO Box 4000, Dallas TX 75208,
or visit us online at *www.TonyEvans.org*.

NOTES

1. Jamie Dean, "Unconquered," *World Magazine*, November 25, 2015, accessed July 6, 2016, https://world.wng .org/2015/11/unconquered?utm_source=hootsuite.

2. "Their God Is My God," The Voice of the Martyrs, April 9, 2015, accessed July 6, 2016, http://www .persecution.com/public/newsroom.aspx?story_ID =%3D373535.

3. Dan Joseph, "Nearly 50 Million Abortions Have Been Performed in U.S. Since Roe v. Wade Decision Legalized Abortion," January 25, 2011, accessed May 28, 2016, http://cnsnews.com/news/article/nearly -50-million-abortions-have-been-performed-us-roe -v-wade-decision-legalized.

4. Matthew 6:19-20; Hebrews 13:5; Luke 12:15; Colossians 3:5; Proverbs 23:21; Ezekiel 16:49-50.

5. Daniel Burke, "Millennials Leaving Churches in Droves," May 14, 2015, accessed July 6, 2016, http:// www.cnn.com/2015/05/12/living/pew-religion -study/; "American's Changing Religious Landscape," Pew Research Center, May 12, 2015, accessed July 6, 2016, http://www.pewforum.org/2015/05 /12/americas-changing-religious-landscape/.

6. "What Difference Does Christianity Make?" Grey Matter Research and Consulting, April 6, 2012, accessed May 28, 2016, http://www.greymatterresearch .com/index_files/Impact.htm.

7. Michael D. Tanner, "More Proof We Can't Stop Poverty by Making It More Comfortable," *Investor's Business Daily*, September 17, 2010.

8. Liz Bowie, "Water from a Fountain? Not in Baltimore Schools," *The Baltimore Sun*, April 9, 2016, accessed May 23, 2016, http://www.baltimoresun .com/news/maryland/baltimore-city/bs-md-ci-lead -in-water-20160409-story.html.

ABOUT THE AUTHOR

DR. TONY EVANS is founder and senior pastor of Oak Cliff Bible Fellowship in Dallas, founder and president of The Urban Alternative, former chaplain of the NFL's Dallas Cowboys, and longstanding chaplain of the NBA's Dallas Mavericks. His radio broadcast, *The Alternative with Dr. Tony Evans,* can be heard on nearly 1,000 US radio outlets daily and in more than 130 countries. Dr. Evans is the prolific author of more than 100 books, booklets, and Bible studies, including the best-selling *Kingdom Man* and *Kingdom Woman* (written with his daughter Chrystal). As a pastor, teacher, author, and speaker, he serves the body of Christ using his unique ability to communicate complex theological truths through simple, yet profound, illustrations.

Meet the rest of the family

Expert advice on parenting and marriage . . .
spiritual growth . . . powerful personal stories . . .

Focus on the Family's collection of inspiring, practical resources can help your family grow closer to God—and each other—than ever before. Whichever format you need—video, audio, book or eBook—we have something for you. Visit our online Family Store and discover how we can help your family thrive at **FocusOnTheFamily.com/store**.

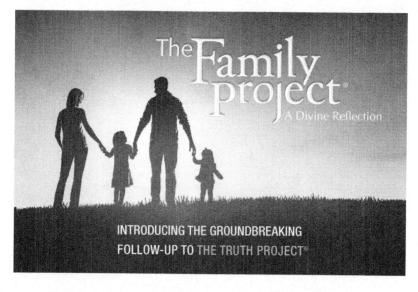

THE PROFOUND IMPACT OF BIBLICAL FAMILIES

From the creators of the life-changing series *The Truth Project®* comes a stunning new journey of discovery that explores family as a revelation of God—and the extraordinary impact families have on the world around them. Introducing *The Family Project®*, a transformative, feature-length documentary and DVD curriculum that reveals—through an in-depth exploration of God's design and purpose—biblical truths about the role of families in society.

CPSIA information can be obtained at www.ICGtesting.com
Printed in the USA
BVOW08s0708270916

462890BV00009B/1/P